# WWI

## NEWS FROM THE TRENCHES

WORLD WAR 100
**Mirror**

Hotel De Ritz

"ONE DAY THE GREAT EUROPEAN WAR WILL COME OUT OF SOME DAMNED FOOLISH THING IN THE BALKANS"

GERMAN CHANCELLOR
OTTO VON BISMARCK (1888)

## Trinity Mirror Media

# WWI NEWS FROM THE TRENCHES

Heritage Editor: Harri Aston

Design: Ben Renshaw

Production: Harri Aston, Claudia Tanner

Head of Syndication and Licensing: Fergus McKenna

Archive Research: Simon Flavin, David Scripps,
Vito Inglese, John Mead, Manjit Sandhu,
Paul Mason, Holly Beckett, Lisa Tomkins

Photography: Mirrorpix, PA Photos

Published by Trinity Mirror Media

Managing Editor: Eugene Duffy
SM Managing Director: Ken Rogers
SM Publishing Director: Steve Hanrahan
SM Commercial Director: Will Beedles
SM Account Manager: Chris Connolly
Executive Art Editor: Rick Cooke
Executive Editor: Paul Dove
Sales & Marketing Manager: Elizabeth Morgan
Senior Marketing Executive: Claire Brown

First Edition
Published in Great Britain in 2014.
Published and produced by: Trinity Mirror Media,
PO Box 48, Old Hall Street, Liverpool L69 3EB.

Acknowledgments
In addition to material from the Daily Mirror archive,
several other sources were used during the production
of this book. They include:

Chapters 1-9
The Imperial War Museum sound archive
Forgotten Voices Of The Great War,
edited by Max Arthur and published by Ebury Press
Forgotten Voices Of The Somme,
edited by Joshua Levine and published by Ebury Press

Chapter 12
John French's diaries,
which are on display at Redruth Old Cornwall Society Museum
Letters From The Front,
by Andrew Roberts, published by Osprey Publishing
A Nurse At The Front, published by Simon & Schuster
A Home Front Diary: 1914-1918, published by Amberley

ISBN: 9781908695925
Printed and bound by Korotan

**Right** Prime Minister David Lloyd George inspects workers
during a visit to a munitions factory in August 1918

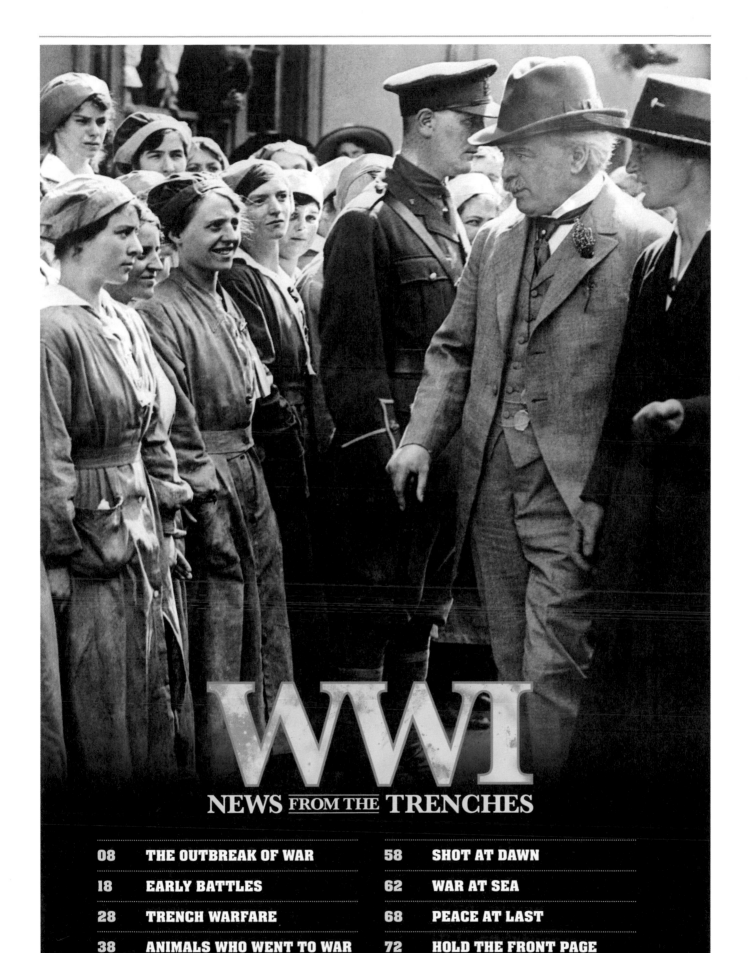

# WWI

## NEWS FROM THE TRENCHES

# LOST AND FOUND: IMAGES, STORIES AND PAGES THAT TELL REAL STORY OF WAR

"Are we on the eve of a terrible European conflict?" the Daily Mirror asked on its front page on July 29, 1914.

It was just a month after the assassination of Archduke Franz Ferdinand, heir to the throne of the Austro-Hungarian Empire, by a Serbian nationalist in Sarajevo.

War was declared on Serbia, whose leaders Austria-Hungary blamed for being complicit in the murder, prompting the Daily Mirror's warning of the possible bloodshed to come.

Our photographers risked their lives to record the resulting horror that unfolded as various alliances dragged most of Europe's countries into war.

Their remarkable images regularly featured on the Daily Mirror's front pages, which told the story of the conflict like no other newspaper.

To mark 100 years since the outbreak of the First World War, we have dug deep into the archives to unearth thousands of lost images, pages and stories which shine a fascinating light on the conflict.

We begin with the story of a teenager who signed up as the country was gripped by patriotic fever and follow the soldiers as they cross the Channel to France and head to the front line for their first brutal encounter with the Germans at the Battle of Mons.

The horror of the first day of the Battle of the Somme is also told through the voices of the men who fought in it, beginning with the nervous soldier who had a "terrible feeling" as he waited for the order to go "over the top".

One of the heroes of the war was a carrier pigeon credited with saving the lives of 194 servicemen, and we explain the role animals played throughout the conflict, from the horses who supplied their comrades with food, water and ammunition, to the dogs who

The Daily Mirror's front page on July 29, 1914, after the declaration of war on Serbia

carried aid to the wounded and took messages between the lines.

We also take a closer look at the Government's propaganda machine, featuring the posters that were designed to encourage men to enlist.

While millions of people went off to fight a battle was also being waged on the home front, and we highlight in particular the role of women during the conflict as they took on jobs the men left behind.

Meanwhile, out on the battlefields, more than 300 British soldiers would die at the hands of their own men.

We tell some of the heartbreaking stories of some of the 'cowards' who fell in front of the firing squad, including two teenagers who

fled just as they were about to take part in their first attack, and include the first-hand experiences of those who had to pull the trigger.

The war was also fought at sea and our feature on the Battle of Jutland provides a vivid account of what happened when the British and German fleets clashed in the only full-scale naval battle of the conflict.

The last British soldier to be killed in action was Private George Ellison, who had fought in the war since the very beginning, and we look at what happened on the day the conflict finally came to an end.

We revisit the famous Christmas truce as we tell the story of the war through the Daily Mirror's groundbreaking front pages,

Crowds gather near Downing Street as members of the Liberal Government, led by Herbert Asquith, discuss the invasion of Belgium by German forces at a Cabinet meeting on August 3, 1914

from Franz Ferdinand's assassination to the day victory finally came after four years of slaughter.

While there would hardly have been a family left untouched by the war, Amy Beechey's suffered more than most, with the widow losing five children in the conflict. The fascinating war diaries Edith Appleton kept of her experiences caring for wounded soldiers are also featured, as are the letters sent home from the front and the exploits of flying ace Edward 'Mick' Mannock.

A century on from one of history's darkest episodes, WWI: News From The Trenches is the story of the war from the very front line.

# 'DON'T YOU MEAN YOU'RE 19? SIGN HERE...'

**Europe was already on a knife edge when Archduke Franz Ferdinand was shot dead in Sarajevo on June 28, 1914. Within weeks the continent's major powers were at war and, in Britain, there was only one question on everybody's lips...**

"**W**hat are you doing about the war?" asked the voice on the other end of the telephone.

Reginald Haine was an articled clerk and had just returned to work after a fortnight's holiday when his friend called.

"I have joined my brother's regiment which is the Honourable Artillery Company," the friend added. "If you like, come along. I can get you in."

Reginald went to the local recruitment centre, where there was a queue of about a thousand people, on his lunch break.

His friend took him right to the front, where a sergeant major was standing next to a desk.

"Are you willing to join?" the officer asked.

"Yes sir," replied Reginald.

The age limit to join the Army was 19 but, with recruitment officers paid a bounty for every new person they enlisted, many were willing to turn a blind eye.

"Well, how old are you?" asked the officer.

"I am 18 and one month."

Volunteers queue to enlist outside a recruiting office in 1914

"Do you mean 19 and one month?"

Reginald thought for a brief moment, then replied: "Yes sir."

"Right-ho, well sign here please."

And that was that. Reginald was off to fight for a country gripped by patriotic fever following the declaration of war against Germany on August 4, 1914.

At the time, the British Army was minuscule in comparison to the conscript-heavy armies on the continent. It comprised just 450,000 men and some 250,000 reservists, compared to the four million or so that Germany could call upon.

War Secretary Lord Kitchener believed the regular army should be used to help train a new army, warning the Government that the conflict would be decided by the last million men that Britain could throw into battle, and he quickly appealed for 100,000 volunteers.

The target was reached in two weeks, with another 650,000 new recruits enlisted by the end of September to take part in a conflict which many believed would be over by Christmas. By that time, a million volunteers had come forward.

"I said to my boss 'I want to join the Army, I want to be released from my job'," said Private F.B. Vaughan as he looked back on his decision to sign up.

"He said to me, 'Here in the steelworks you are doing just as much for your country, just as much for the nation, as though you were in the Army'.

"Well, I couldn't see myself catching the 8.40 every morning and leaving for home in the afternoon, doing little jobs in the evening, and all the time my pals were suffering – probably dying somewhere. I couldn't see myself carrying on in that particular way, so I said 'I'm awfully sorry but I have made my mind up, I must go'."

Among those who thought they were signing up for an exciting adventure was Thomas McIndoe, who went to a recruitment centre for the Middlesex Regiment after seeing the famous call-to-arms poster featuring Kitchener and his pointing finger.

# BRITONS

"WANTS

# YOU"

## JOIN YOUR COUNTRY'S ARMY!

### GOD SAVE THE KING

Reproduced by permission of LONDON OPINION

The famous poster in which War Secretary Lord Kitchener appeals for volunteers to join the Army

"I was always a tall and fairly fit lad," he recalled.

"When I confronted the recruiting officer he said that I was too young, although I had said that I was 18 years of age. He said, 'Well, I think you are too young son. Come back in another year or so'. I returned home and never said anything to my parents.

"I picked up my bowler hat, which my mother had bought me and which was only to wear on Sundays, and I donned that thinking it would make me look older.

"I presented myself to the recruiting officer again, and this time there was no queries,

June 28 Assassination of Archduke Franz Ferdinand, heir to the throne of Austro-Hungarian empire in Sarajevo

July 28 Austria-Hungary declares war on Serbia

July 30 Russia begins to mobilise forces

August 1 Germany declares war on Russia

August 3 Germany declares war on France, German troops enter Belgium

August 4 Britain declares war on Germany*

August 5 France declares war on Germany

August 6 Austria-Hungary declares war on Russia

* Britain had promised to defend Belgium's neutrality under the Treaty of London, signed in 1839

I was accepted. Birth certificates were not asked of. I was 16 in the June."

William Dove had just finished watching a movie being screened at Shepherd's Bush Empire in London when a short film came on. It showed a navy fleet sailing the high seas, while songs such as Rule Britannia and Heart Of Oak were played to further stir patriotic spirits.

"You know one feels that little shiver run up the back and you know you have got to do something," William recalled. "I had just turned 17 at that time and on the Monday I went up to Whitehall – Old Scotland Yard – and enlisted in the 16th Lancers."

Some people consulted the Bible as they considered whether taking part in the war would contradict their religious beliefs. Among them was Godfrey Bloom.

"It was interesting to find out how many battles in the Old Testament were 'by the word of the Lord'. And in the New Testament neither John the Baptist nor Our Lord ever said anything against a soldier – only told them to do their job within the limits of war.

## ❝ONE FEELS THAT LITTLE SHIVER RUN UP THE BACK AND YOU KNOW YOU HAVE TO DO SOMETHING❞

"These things in my young mind built up to a confidence that if death was abroad, if wrong was to be resisted, a Christian should be right in amongst it."

Before going on the battlefield, a new recruit would have to undergo 12 weeks of training where they would learn how to dig trenches and use a bayonet.

"Fixing bayonets is one of the most wonderful things in the Army," said Pte Vaughan as he recalled his military training.

"The sergeant major was telling the troops how to fix bayonets, and he said, 'When I says fix, you don't fix, but when I says bayonets you whips 'em out and whops 'em on.' And that was the style of some of our sergeants and sergeant-majors who had been old sweats in the Boer War. They were fine chaps."

Rifleman Henry Williamson's preparations for the war were gruelling. He was forced to carry 60lb of ammunition, kit and a rifle for up to 16 miles each day.

Men reading the mobilisation proclamation, which is pictured right

Recruiting sergeants try to sign up volunteers who have just watched The Life Of A Soldier at the Angel Picture Theatre in London

Army Form D. 427.

# GENERAL MOBILIZATION
# Army Reserve

## (REGULAR AND SPECIAL RESERVISTS).

HIS MAJESTY THE KING has been graciously pleased to direct by Proclamation that the Army Reserve be called out on permanent service.

**ALL REGULAR RESERVISTS** are required to report themselves at once at their place of joining in accordance with the instructions on their identity certificates for the purpose of joining the Army.

**ALL SPECIAL RESERVISTS** are required to report themselves on such date and at such places as they may be directed to attend for the purpose of joining the Army. If they have not received any such directions, or if they have changed their address since last attendance at drill or training, they will report themselves at once, by letter, to the Adjutant of their Unit or Depot.

The necessary instructions as to their joining will then be given.

"We lay on our backs gasping, water bottles were drunk dry," he remembered. "We passed some of the battalions who had been in front of us and I remember so well the dead white faces, many with boils, lying completely exhausted, sun stricken in the hedges, hundreds of them."

Special train services were put on to transport tens of thousands of men from across the country to Southampton, from where most of the soldiers would set sail.

On August 9, the first ships carrying members of the British Expeditionary Force left for France, where 80,000 would head over the following week to the ports of Boulogne, Le Havre and Rouen.

A personal message was issued to every man from Lord Kitchener, reminding him

**Above and left**
Huge crowds of people turn up at a recruiting station at Scotland Yard, London, in the days following the outbreak of war

to do his duty, be on his best behaviour and resist the temptation of "wine and women".

Shortly before setting off, Fusilier William Holbrook was waiting on a beach on the Isle of Wight when he saw a placard on the side of a house advertising a magazine, alongside the words 'The Dawn of Britain's Greatest Glory'.

"I was lying there and I thought to myself, I wonder whether it will be or not."

A few days after arriving in France, William was on his way to Belgium, where he would be part of the Allied effort to hold the line of the Mons–Conde Canal against the advancing German army.

"We went on a cattle-truck type train, eight horses and 40 men. We marched from there to the front – of course we did not know where we were going, and the whole brigade came together.

"Before we got to Mons we went through a place called Frameries, a mining town about 10 miles from Mons.

"It was wonderful there, the people came out and cheered and shouted, and gave us food and a tremendous welcome."

They were about to discover the Germans were planning a very different reception, one which would give the British their first bloody taste of the war.

# " IT WAS WONDERFUL, THE PEOPLE CAME OUT AND CHEERED AND SHOUTED, AND GAVE US FOOD AND A TREMENDOUS WELCOME "

Horatio Bottomley, a former Liberal MP who owned the rabble-rousing magazine John Bull, is pictured making a speech at a recruitment event in Trafalgar Square in 1914

# Pals serving together on the battlefield

With the British Army vastly outnumbered compared to its European neighbours, manpower was needed and it was needed fast.

It was thought men would more readily enlist if they could serve with their friends, neighbours and work colleagues, rather than being arbitrarily allocated to regiments.

And so office clerks, factory workers and messenger boys came together for the 'Pals' battalions' in a surge of patriotic fervour.

In August 1914, Major General Sir Henry Rawlinson appealed to London stockbrokers to set an example.

Within a week, 1,600 men enlisted in the 10th Battalion Royal Fusiliers, the so-called 'Stockbrokers' Battalion'.

Lord Derby, known as "England's best recruiting sergeant", coined the term 'pals' when he was recruiting in

The Manchester Pals on a parade in 1915

Liverpool. Volunteers were asked to turn up at the headquarters of the King's Liverpool Regiment on August 28, 1914. The sheer number of men who showed up overwhelmed the recruiting hall, and extra rooms had to be opened to deal with them.

Many similar Pals' battalions were formed. While they undoubtedly boosted numbers and camaraderie, if such units

suffered heavy casualties in battle, it meant that small communities would be particularly hard hit.

The Pals would go on to fight in some of the most costly battles of the First World War, taking part in the 'big push' at the Somme in 1916.

When tragedy struck, whole streets would lose their menfolk overnight.

Soldiers from the 6th (Service) Battalion of the King's Liverpool Regiment learn how to use their bayonets against the enemy during a training exercise

British troops leaving the French port Boulogne, bound for Belgium and the front line to stop the German advance

British troops gather outside the railway station in Ostend, Belgium, prior to setting off to the front in September 1914

British soldiers on their way across the Channel to France in August 1914

A Prussian Guard band heads a column of troops marching through the streets of Berlin

A crowd looks on as two policemen post a mobilisation order in Berlin

# HUNGRY, EXHAUSTED AND FIGHTING FOR THEIR LIVES

**Staying alive in the heat of battle was tiring work, as one soldier was able to testify after facing the enemy for the first time...**

**"WE HAD TO GUARD THEM ALL NIGHT. THEY SLEPT NICELY ON STRAW WHILE WE HAD TO GUARD THEM AND GIVE THEM HALF OUR RATIONS!"**

Enjoying the company of villagers several miles from the front line, the order suddenly came for Gunner Walter Burchmore to mount his horse and prepare for action.

Coming in on high ground overlooking the Belgian city of Mons, he caught his first sight of the enemy and, almost immediately, began exchanging fire.

"It was quite obvious that the Germans didn't intend to give us any rest and we quite made up our mind that we wouldn't give them any rest either," remembered Walter, a member of the Royal Horse Artillery.

After some fierce fighting, in which Walter's team inflicted heavy losses on the Germans, the order came for the British to try to retake Binche.

"The battle went on for several hours and I thought that we were going to take the place but I doubt very much whether we could have held it if we had.

"We were completely exhausted, thoroughly hungry, and I don't think we were capable of any reasonable further movement. There was only one thing that managed to keep us going and that was the knowledge we were fighting for our very lives."

They were eventually forced to retreat from Mons due to the greater strength of the Germans and the sudden withdrawal of the French 5th Army, which exposed the British right flank.

The retreat lasted for two weeks and took the British to the outskirts of Paris before they counter-attacked alongside the French at the Battle of the Marne.

Sergeant Thomas Painting and his men were forbidden to carry white handkerchiefs in case they were used as white flags but it was actually the Germans who were about to surrender in large numbers.

"We went in as we had been trained – one section would advance under covering fire of another section, leapfrogging each other as the others were firing to keep Jerry's heads down," recalled Sgt Painting.

"My company was going in with their bayonets when suddenly Jerry put up a white flag.

"We took 540 prisoners. I said to one of them, 'Why did you pack up when you've got so much ammunition?'

"He said, 'Well, your fire was so accurate we couldn't put our heads up to shoot at you'. We lost 12 killed and 60 wounded, they had lost about 180 men.

"We had to guard them all night. They slept nicely on straw while we had to guard them and give them half our rations!"

Following a decisive Allied victory, the so-called 'Race to the Sea' began, as each army attempted to outflank the other on their way northwards. The race ended in mid-October at Ypres, with its fortifications guarding the ports of the English Channel and access to the North Sea and beyond.

Private Clifford Lane was on board one of the open-topped buses carrying hundreds of soldiers towards the front line when a bright autumn day took a turn for the worse.

He was thoroughly soaked by the time he reached his destination, Vlamertinge, where a generous supply of rum was available to help lift spirits before the soldiers went on the march.

Passing a Roman Catholic priest who removed his hat and murmured his blessings, the Tommies spent a cold night in a field. In the morning, they were told to go up a wooded hillside, where they found dugouts in which they could rest more comfortably.

From there, they could see a road running towards Ypres, where they spotted a group of French soldiers.

"While we were watching there was the sound of heavy gunfire and, after a few seconds, three violent explosions," Pte Clifford remembered.

"When the smoke cleared we saw this group picking up one of their number and immediately start to dig a grave for him, so the shell had killed him. That was the first time we realised what the war was about – what the Germans could do."

## "THE WINTER OF '14 WAS EXTREMELY HARD BECAUSE WE HAD NO AMENITIES WHATSOEVER"

**Left** British soldiers waiting to fire on enemy from behind barbed wire, somewhere in northern France, in September 1914

**Above** British soldiers firing a machine gun from behind a hedge in the snow in December 1914

The arrival of winter forced the battle to a halt. By this time, the trenches were often "just waterlogged ditches", recalled Pte Reginald Haine.

"Practically the whole time you had to sleep with your boots on in case things went wrong anywhere.

"Even if one was in support – not in reserve so much, in reserve you could get your clothes off – but if you were in support you had to sleep in your clothes.

"The winter of '14 was extremely hard because we had no amenities whatsoever. One was often up to one's knees in frozen mud. You could do nothing about it except stick there."

The soldiers would end up sticking there for another four years, although they were not to know this at the time.

"A lot of people thought it would be over by Christmas," said Pte Tom Adlam, of the Hampshire Regiment.

"I was never one of those who thought that at the beginning. But I put it down about a year. I think most of us thought it would last about a year. We thought it couldn't go on longer than that."

Kaiser Wilhelm II, far right, is pictured with high-ranking German officers observing army

Belgian troops respond to the German shelling near Antwerp in September 1914

# First Briton to die in the war 'was only 16'

The first British soldier to die in the First World War was thought to be just 16 years old.

Private John Parr's age is listed as 20 in the official cemetery register – but like many keen young recruits he most probably lied about his age when he joined up in 1913.

The young golf caddy, from Finchley, North London, joined the Middlesex Regiment and was soon sent to the Western Front.

It is believed he and another recruit were sent on bikes to the village of Obourg, just north east of Mons, on a mission to locate the enemy on August 21, 1914.

The pair met a German cavalry patrol and John was shot as he tried to hold off the enemy while his companion went to report back.

Because British troops retreated to a new position, the teenager's body was left behind and his death was not officially reported until a year later.

No picture of him has ever been found and relatives have come forward to suggest his family at the time were so devastated by their loss that his name was rarely mentioned thereafter.

In an extraordinary coincidence, John's grave faces that of George Ellison – the last soldier to die in the war – in Belgium's Saint Symphorien cemetery.

**Above** The grave of John Parr, the first British soldier to die in the war

Belgian soldiers shelter in a trench beside a railway line at the Battle of Hofstade.
Shells bursting over them, they lost all four of their commanders

**Left** British marines are seen here sniping at the enemy from the windows of houses on a road two miles from the outskirts of Antwerp

**Right** British troops take up defensive positions in a trench during the early weeks of the war

# Cousins at war

During the First World War, the three ruling monarchs of Britain, Germany and Russia were all related – yet could not have been more divided.

King George V of Britain and Kaiser Wilhelm II of Germany were both grandsons of Queen Victoria, while the mothers of George and the Tsar were sisters.

The men ruled three of the most powerful states in the world, yet as Europe plunged into war, their inability to curtail international hostilities was apparent.

Wilhelm was arrogant and lived a life of frivolity.

He loved all things military but his understanding of such matters was superficial and his generals bypassed him.

Following his forced abdication after the war, Wilhelm lived in exile in the Netherlands. George described him as "the greatest criminal known".

Meanwhile, Nicholas ruled with absolute power over his people.

Despite having no experience, he took personal command of the military, which proved a fatal error.

When he was forced to abdicate, King George refused him asylum, afraid of the public's reaction if the fallen Tsar came to Britain.

On July 18, 1918, Nicholas was shot by the Bolsheviks.

King George preferred stamp collecting to intellectual matters.

David Lloyd George said of him: "The King is a very jolly chap . . . thank God there is not much in his head."

Of the three cousins, George wielded the least power but was the only one to survive in post.

Family ties stood for little as the rulers were at the mercy of more powerful forces: the generals, politicians, imperial expansion, national pride and military glory.

From left, King George V, Germany's Kaiser Wilhelm II and Tsar Nicholas II of Russia

# THE WORLD AT WAR

Europe was split into two rival camps, the Central Powers led by Germany and Austria-Hungary, and the Allied Powers of Britain, France and Russia. The coloured map shows which side each country eventually chose to support during the conflict, as well as the estimated strength of each army in 1914

**UNITED KINGDOM**
**700,000**

London

Mons

Paris

**FRANCE**
**3,600,000**

**KEY**

| ALLIES | CENTRAL POWERS | NEUTRAL |

**ITALY**
**1,500,000**

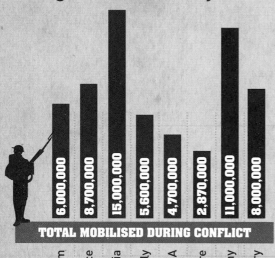

**TOTAL MOBILISED DURING CONFLICT**

| United Kingdom | France | Russia | Italy | USA | Ottoman Empire | Germany | Austria-Hungary |
|---|---|---|---|---|---|---|---|
| 6,000,000 | 8,700,000 | 15,000,000 | 5,600,000 | 4,700,000 | 2,870,000 | 11,000,000 | 8,000,000 |

**KEY FIGURES**

**Franz Ferdinand**

• The assassinated heir to the throne of Austria-Hungary.

**Kaiser Wilhelm II**

• The German Emperor and King of Prussia.

**King George V**

• Britain's monarch from 1910 until his death in 1936.

**Tsar Nicholas II**

• Russian ruler until his enforced abdication in 1917.

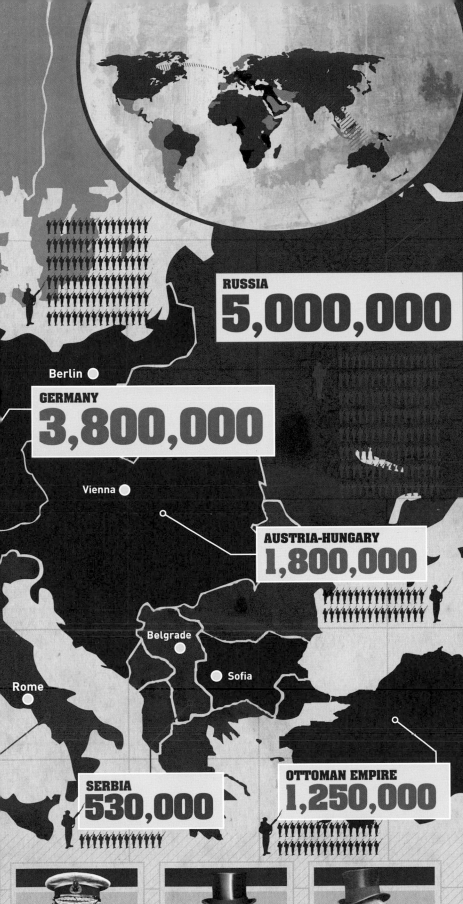

**RUSSIA**
# 5,000,000

**GERMANY**
# 3,800,000

Berlin

Vienna

**AUSTRIA-HUNGARY**
# 1,800,000

Belgrade

Sofia

Rome

**SERBIA**
# 530,000

**OTTOMAN EMPIRE**
# 1,250,000

**Lord Kitchener**

- Appointed Secretary of State for War at the outset of the conflict.

**David Lloyd George**

- Appointed Minister of Munitions in 1915 before becoming PM.

**Herbert Asquith**

- Britain's Prime Minister from 1908 until 1916.

## The first six months

**June 28, 1914**
Archduke Franz Ferdinand, heir to the throne of the Austro-Hungarian Empire, and his wife Sophie are assassinated in Sarajevo, Bosnia.

**June 29**
Serbian government accused of complicity in the assassination.

**July 20**
Austria-Hungary sends troops to the Serbian frontier.

**July 25**
Russia arranges for troops to be stationed on Russo-Austrian frontier.

**July 28**
Austria-Hungary declares war on Serbia.

**August 1**
French military mobilisation ordered.
Germany declares war on Russia.
Italy announces neutrality.

**August 3**
Germany declares war on France.
Great Britain gives order for troops to mobilise.

**August 4**
Germany declares war on Belgium.
United States declares neutrality.
Great Britain declares war on Germany and Austria-Hungary.

**August 7**
First members of the British Expeditionary Force (BEF) land in France.

**August 20**
Brussels is evacuated as Germans occupy the city.

**August 23**
The Battle of Mons, the first major action of the BEF in the war.

**September 6**
The First Battle of Marne checks German advance at the cost of 13,000 British lives.

**October 19**
First Battle of Ypres.

**October 29**
The Ottoman Empire enters the war.

**November 22**
Trenches are established along the entire Western Front.

**December 16**
The German First High Sea fleet bombards Hartlepool, Whitby and Scarborough, killing 137 civilians.

# 'I GAVE THE MEN MY LAST ORDERS... TEN SECONDS TO GO, GET READY... OVER!'

## The 'big push' on July 1, 1916, was meant to bring an end to nearly two years of trench warfare but, for the soldiers about to take part in the attack, the tension was difficult to bear...

British soldiers in a communication trench just before an attack was launched during the opening phase of the Battle of the Somme in July 1916

**I**n need of some 'Dutch courage' to calm his nerves, Albert gladly drank the rum that was offered to him.

It was shortly before 7.30am and he was about to climb out of the trenches and go 'over the top' to charge the enemy lines.

"The fact that the others were there kept you going – but I had a terrible feeling..."

Albert Day was one of about 150,000 British soldiers waiting for the whistle that would signal the start of the Battle of the Somme. It was originally intended to be a 'knockout blow' to end the Western Front stalemate in a war that had already lasted two years. The plan was to break through the German line along a 12-mile front north and south of the River Somme in southern France.

The offensive was due to take place on August 1, 1916, but was brought forward a month to relieve pressure on the French, who were suffering heavy losses fighting the Germans at Verdun.

As the countdown to the attack began,

the tension in the trenches was almost unbearable.

"Five minutes before the time of going over ... this was the worst time for the troops. That's when their feelings might break," recalled Lieutenant Ulick Burke of the Devonshire Regiment.

"I gave the men my last orders. They had ladders to help them to climb out of the trench. I shouted down the left and right of my sector, 'five minutes to go!' Then four minutes, then three minutes, two minutes, half a minute, then, 'Ten seconds...get ready... Over!'"

Allied artillery had pounded enemy lines for a week before the attack, in the belief this would break their defences and ensure a rapid advance, but many of the British shells failed to explode.

The German dugouts were also well constructed and heavily fortified, with soldiers able to shelter in underground bunkers in relative safety during the bombardment.

When the shelling ended, the Germans left their bunkers and set up their positions, ready to mow down British troops with their machine guns.

"We were told that the wire had been cut in front of our front line, that there's be no difficulty at all for us to get through and that there wouldn't be a German within miles," recalled Corporal A. Wood of the West Yorkshire Regiment.

"We went up the ladder, on top of the parapet, and immediately anyone appeared, the blast of the machine guns knocked them back into the trench.

"There were Germans sat on the parapet of their trench with machine guns, mowing us down. In fact, I don't think half a dozen of our people got beyond our front line, never mind to the German front line."

British commanders had previously been so confident of success that they ordered their troops to walk slowly towards the German lines. Once they had been seized, cavalry units would pour through to pursue the fleeing Germans.

"We had been led to believe by 'higher-ups' that the big bombardment, over the days and nights, had obliterated the enemy. But we knew it hadn't because their positions were so strong," said Private Frank Lindlay.

"Their dugouts were way down under the parapets of the trenches, and they couldn't be reached by artillery fire. All they did was to wait down there until our barrage lifted,

**Top** Soldiers go 'over the top' in June 1916 to attack the German trenches somewhere in France

**Above** British soldiers take cover during the bombardment of the German lines before the start of the Battle of the Somme. However, around a third of the shells failed to explode and the Germans were able to shelter in heavily-fortified underground bunkers and then they came up to have some target practice at us.

"We were held up by huge coils of barbed wire and, in the odd gap that we made for, we were greeted by their heavy machine guns. There was no question that we could get through to them. Whole lines of our lads were mown down after the other, and we were shifting from shell-hole to shell-hole, trying to pick one or two Germans off their front line."

The British miscalculation was evident almost immediately, with some soldiers quickly being told to retreat back to their bases, as Private Reginald Glenn explained.

"The signal to attack was a whistle. The officers were the first to jump up – and they only had revolvers. We had a creeping barrage that was supposed to be creeping forward as we moved forward.

"The first line went, and then they all lay down. I thought they must have had different orders to us – we'd been told to walk. But the reason they lay down was because they'd been shot. They were mown down like corn.

## "I USED TO GO TO CHURCH WHEN I WAS A LAD BUT I PRAYED MORE IN THAT SHELL-HOLE THAN I EVER PRAYED IN CHURCH"

"Then we went forward – and the same thing happened. I didn't know what was happening around me. I didn't get as far as the British wire.

"There was so much pandemonium. I lay down but soon we all got orders to get back to our trenches."

With his comrades "dropping like ninepins", Private Donald Cameron started praying for survival after finding cover in a shell-hole.

"It must have been about eight o'clock," he remembered.

"The firing went on, and we kept peeping up, looking over the top to check, and the bloody Germans were sniping our wounded. They couldn't see us in our shell-hole.

"I must have prayed a dozen times. I used to go to church when I was a lad but I prayed more in that shell-hole than I ever prayed in church."

A British Grenadier Guardsman keeps watch as his comrades sleep in a captured German trench at Ovillers, near Albert, during the Battle of the Somme in 1916

British soldiers were being massacred on an unprecedented scale. For those lucky enough to survive, like Private Harold Startin, the horrific sights they saw would never leave them. Describing having to bury some of his fallen comrades, he recalled: "If they were lying face downwards it wasn't too bad but if they were lying with their face up, and the sun had been shining on them, the faces were smothered in flies and bluebottles and it was enough to make you sick.

"There were no graves dug for them – they were put into shallows. You might get three, four, five or six into the crater and then you shovel down earth with a spade, and cover the bodies up. There were no crosses put there. We had no wood, we had no nails, we had no hammer. So they were just covered up and left."

For Private Jack Cousins, of the Bedfordshire Regiment, it was a question of "kill or be killed" but one incident in particular disturbed him.

Recalling hearing moans after throwing a grenade into a German dugout, he said: "I took a chance. I went down into the dugout, and there was this Jerry laid with a great hole in his chest, blood pouring everywhere, pointing to his mouth. I knew what he wanted. He wanted a drink. I handed him my water bottle. The water went in his mouth, and came out of his holes.

"He was gone in a few seconds. It really upset me, I felt morally responsible for his death. It could have happened to me."

For the wounded, the pain was sometimes too much to bear.

"One fellow asked me to shoot him," recalled Second Lieutenant W. J. Brockman of the Lancashire Fusiliers. "He was half in and half out of a shell-hole, hopelessly wounded. But I didn't do it. I put his rifle on the ground and put his tin hat on top of it, hoping that somebody wound find him."

Sergeant James Payne, of the Manchester Regiment, was attacking a German trench when his teeth were blown out after he was shot through the cheek.

"I fell forward and spat all my teeth out," he recalled. "I collapsed and, hours later, I came round. My left eye was closed. I couldn't talk. I could breathe, that was all.

"I could see through my right eye and I saw one of my corporals who'd been shot through the foot. We saw a man. A shell had come over and hit him and knocked his left arm and his left leg. His left eye was hanging on his cheek, and he was calling out, 'Annie!' I shot

The bodies of dead German soldiers following the British assault on Guillemont in September 1916

A wounded soldier is carried away on a stretcher during the opening phase of the Battle of the Somme

him. I had to. Put him out of his misery. It hurt me. It hurt me."

At the end of the day 19,000 British soldiers lay dead and another 38,000 were missing or wounded. For these enormous losses all the British had gained was a section of the German front line in the south. Nothing at all had been secured in the north.

"If I said the morale was high I'd be telling a lie," said Corporal Bill Partridge about the mood back at his camp at the end of that day.

"We didn't want to be mutilated – that was our main thought. That, and smoking a cigarette, and wondering if it was going to be the last one."

Lieutenant Burke, who had earlier given the order for his men to attack, added: "There was frustration. We'd lost so many people, and taken so little ground. And men began to wonder, 'Why'. There was no feeling of giving up, they were just wondering 'why?'."

The Somme battle lasted another 140 days and, while none was as bloody as the first day, more than one million men would end up wounded or killed on all sides.

Another major effort to break the deadlock came in September when the British unleashed their secret weapon – the tank.

However, lightly armed, small in number and often subject to mechanical failure, they made little impact.

"Everybody was staggered to see this extraordinary monster crawling over the ground," recalled Captain Philip Neame of

> **"THERE WERE TIMES, AFTER BEING SHELLED FOR HOURS ON END, THAT ALL I WANTED WAS TO BE BLOWN TO BITS"**

British soldiers negotiate a shell-cratered winter landscape after the end of the Allied offensive on the Somme

the Royal Engineers. "Everyone thought it was terrific until the first battle, and then we rather lost faith because it broke down before it reached the German front line. I think we all thought and hoped that the war was bound to end with some form of open warfare. It could not go on forever with this trench warfare."

The strain of fighting in a seemingly endless war would take its toll on many a soldier, as Corporal Clifford Lane explained.

"There were times, after being shelled for hours on end during the latter part of the Somme battle, that all I wanted was to be blown to bits. You know that if you got wounded, they could never get you away, not under these conditions.

"You'd see other people with internal wounds and you thought your only hope was to get killed outright, your only relief. It wasn't only me who felt like that, it happened to lots of people. I suppose we were despondent because after two years the strain was terrific."

Torrential rains in October turned the battlefields into a muddy quagmire and, on November 18, the battle was called off, with the Allies having advanced only five miles.

"No-one can describe what the Battle of the Somme was like unless they were there," said Private H.D. Jackson of the Royal Army Medical Corps. "It was one continuous stream of wounded and dead and dying."

A wounded man being carried across a sunken road after the attack at Beaumont-Hamel on the first day of the Somme campaign

**Left** An Army chaplain tending to a British soldier's grave

**Below** Scottish soldiers are prepared for a gas attack near the River Somme in 1916

# SOMME

The Battle of the Somme was waged along a 25-mile front, with Britain leading the offensive and France providing some support in the south. The map shows the key battleground areas and the progress made by the Allies over a period of five months.

**June 24, 1916**

The Allies begin a week-long artillery bombardment of German defensive positions on the Somme River.

**July 1**

Around 19,000 British soldiers are killed on the first day of the Battle of the Somme.

**July 13**

The British launch a night attack along a 3.5-mile section of the front. After advancing nearly 1,000 yards, the advance

## BATTLEFIELD KEY 1916

| | |
|---|---|
| ALLIED TROOPS | GERMAN TROOPS |
| ALLIED FRONT | GERMAN FRONT |
| ALLIED SHELLING | NO MAN'S LAND |

### Battlefield weapons

Bapaume

River Ancre

Serre

Beaumont-Hamel

Poziéres

Thiepval

Montauban

56 Div.

48 Div.

31 Div.

4 Div.

29 Div.

36 Div.

32 Div.

8 Div.

34 Div.

30 D

18 Div.

7 Div.

9 Div.

FOURTH ARMY
Albert

21 Div.

17 Div.

**TANK**
Tanks were used in action for the first time on September 15, 1916, during the Battle of the Somme and developed by the British in a bid to end the stalemate on the Western Front.

**MACHINE GUN**
The machine gun was a fearsome defensive weapon capable of firing hundreds of rounds per minute, with many soldiers barely getting out of their trench before they were cut down.

HAZARD!

**POISON GAS**
Chlorine gas was first used by the Germans in Ypres in 1915. Phosgene – a similar but more potent agent which destroys victims' respiratory organs – and mustard gas – a blistering agent that attacks the skin, eyes and lungs, were also used during the war.

**TRENCH MORTAR**
Fired from the relative safety of a trench, it was designed to fire shells at relatively short range, but with a high trajectory, so that they would land directly on top of the enemy trenches.

**FLAME THROWER**
The flamethrower was a powerful, demoralising weapon that caused terror on the battlefield. It was first used by the Germans during the Battle of Verdun in February 1915. Britain and France both adopted the weapon later on.

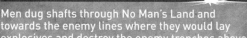

## TUNNELLERS

Men dug shafts through No Man's Land and towards the enemy lines where they would lay explosives and destroy the enemy trenches above.

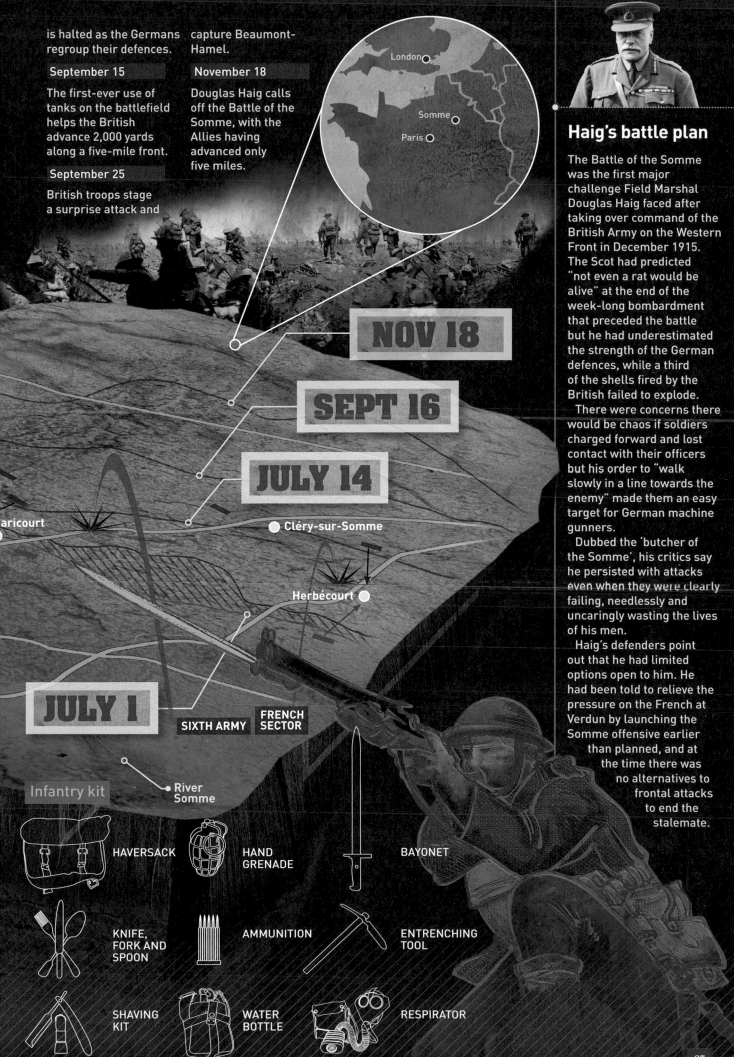

is halted as the Germans regroup their defences.

**September 15**

The first-ever use of tanks on the battlefield helps the British advance 2,000 yards along a five-mile front.

**September 25**

British troops stage a surprise attack and

capture Beaumont-Hamel.

**November 18**

Douglas Haig calls off the Battle of the Somme, with the Allies having advanced only five miles.

London

Somme

Paris

**NOV 18**

**SEPT 16**

**JULY 14**

aricourt

Cléry-sur-Somme

Herbécourt

**JULY 1**

SIXTH ARMY | FRENCH SECTOR

Infantry kit

River Somme

## Haig's battle plan

The Battle of the Somme was the first major challenge Field Marshal Douglas Haig faced after taking over command of the British Army on the Western Front in December 1915. The Scot had predicted "not even a rat would be alive" at the end of the week-long bombardment that preceded the battle but he had underestimated the strength of the German defences, while a third of the shells fired by the British failed to explode.

There were concerns there would be chaos if soldiers charged forward and lost contact with their officers but his order to "walk slowly in a line towards the enemy" made them an easy target for German machine gunners.

Dubbed the 'butcher of the Somme', his critics say he persisted with attacks even when they were clearly failing, needlessly and uncaringly wasting the lives of his men.

Haig's defenders point out that he had limited options open to him. He had been told to relieve the pressure on the French at Verdun by launching the Somme offensive earlier than planned, and at the time there was no alternatives to frontal attacks to end the stalemate.

HAVERSACK

HAND GRENADE

BAYONET

KNIFE, FORK AND SPOON

AMMUNITION

ENTRENCHING TOOL

SHAVING KIT

WATER BOTTLE

RESPIRATOR

# ANIMALS SENT INTO THE LINE OF FIRE

**The First World War was a conflict which pitched as many animals into battle as it did humans. And, as one soldier discovered, they were no less valuable...**

**T**he horses' lives were the first to be saved, as Norman Booth discovered when gas masks started arriving on the front line.

In the event of a chemical attack, he and his fellow Tommies were ordered to put the equipment on the steeds before trying to save themselves.

"We were told it cost £50 for a horse but only a King's shilling to sign up another soldier," Norman recalled.

In the mud, rain and terror of the trenches the war horses supplied their comrades with food, water and ammunition, and also brought back the wounded on stretchers placed on carriages. This meant they would be caught up in mustard gas attacks, get stuck on the barbed wire in front of the trenches and be left injured in No Man's Land.

"Dead horses were simply buried in the mud," said Norman, who served as a groomsman in the Duke of Wellington's Regiment.

"Then an order came out to save the horses' hides and eventually we whipped off the whole buttocks which were then cooked. If it was a young horse you were all right but the older ones tended to be a bit tough. We didn't care as long as we had something to eat."

Of the million horses sent overseas to help with the war effort, only 62,000 returned home. It was a conflict that pitched as many animals into the line of fire as it did humans.

Without them, the ability of the British Army to wage war would have been nigh-on impossible.

Elizabeth Owen, a seven-year-old schoolgirl on the outbreak of war, remembered the "khaki men" who came to take away all the horses from her village.

"Everything in the village was done by horses," she said. "The station was about a mile or a mile-and-a-half away and the train was met by a brake drawn by horses. The milk was delivered by horses and the butter used to be collected from the farms and brought in by horses to the butter market.

"There was a farmer who had a lovely pair who we called the prancers. He thought he would try and hide these horses but the khaki men found them. They tied them all together on a long rope, I think there was about 20 – all the horses we used to know and love and feed. Then they started trotting them out of the village and, as they went out of sight, we were all terribly sad."

Despite their strength, the horses were no less vulnerable to the dangers of the battlefield.

"Heaving about in the filthy mud of the road was an unfortunate mule with both of his forelegs shot away," Lieutenant R. G. Dixon, of the Royal Garrison Artillery, recorded in his diary. "The poor brute, suffering God knows what untold agonies and terrors, was trying desperately to get to its feet which weren't there.

"Jerry's shells were arriving pretty fast – we made some desperate attempts to get to the mule so that I could put a bullet behind its ear into the brain but to no avail. The shelling got more intense – perhaps one would hit the poor thing and put it out of its misery."

Even horses belonging to higher ranks were not spared the horrors of the front line.

General Jack Seely, famed for his heroics at the battle at Moreuil Wood where he led the charge on the back of his trusted horse Warrior, said of the steed: "He had to endure everything most hateful to him – violent noise, the bursting of great shells and bright flashes at night, when the white light of bursting shells must have caused violent pain to such sensitive eyes as horses possess.

"Above all, the smell of blood, terrifying to every horse. Many people do not realise how acute is his sense of smell but most will have read his terror when he smells blood."

Up to 20,000 dogs were also trained for frontline duties during the war, carrying aid to the wounded, taking messages between the lines and sniffing out enemy soldiers.

They were also used for pulling machine guns and equipment, while sentinel dogs were trained to stand quietly on the top of the trench alongside their master's gun barrel, in order to let the soldiers know if anyone attempted to approach the barbed wire.

More than 100,000 pigeons were used to send messages to and from the front line while caged canaries, being the first to die from the effects of poison gas, were also kept in the trenches to act as an early warning system against a chemical attack.

**Opposite** Horses and men in gas masks during tests to find the best protection against chemical attacks

**Below** Cavalry crossing a bridge above a trench, with troops walking underneath, in 1917

# The pigeon who saved the lives of nearly 200 men

Among the heroes of the war was a carrier pigeon credited with saving the lives of 194 servicemen.

Hundreds of soldiers from Major Charles Whittlesey's battalion found themselves trapped on a hillside behind enemy lines without food or ammunition, and were also beginning to receive friendly fire from Allied troops who did not know their location.

Whittlesey sent carrier pigeons to deliver notes asking for help. Two pigeons were shot down before the last pigeon available, Cher Ami ("dear friend" in French), was dispatched.

The note read: "We are along the road parallel to 276.4. Our own artillery is dropping a barrage directly on us. For heaven's sake, stop it!"

During his flight, Cher Ami was shot through the breast, blinded in one eye and his left leg was hanging on by a tendon but he still delivered the note, clutched in his left claw.

After the battle, Army medics saved Cher Ami and carved a small wooden leg for him.

The pigeon was proclaimed a war hero upon his return to America. He was awarded the French Croix de Guerre award for his heroic service and was inducted into the Racing Pigeon Hall of Fame.

He died in 1919, likely as a result of his battle wounds, and his body is on display at the National Museum of American History in Washington.

**Above** Goats provided these soldiers, from the 3rd Lahore Indian Division in France, with milk and meat in 1914

**Left** A camel being given a drink of water in 1916

**Left** British cavalry watering their horses in a captured French village in 1917

**Below** Belgian cavalry on a training exercise in November 1915

**Above** A trench messenger dog delivers news to a British trench on the Western Front in 1918

A French Red Cross dog is seen here scaling a 6ft-high wall in 1916

British cavalry watering their horses at a river in France in October 1914

Horses are lowered down in a sling onto the quayside at
Salonika as they arrive in Greece in 1915

# THE BATTLE TO WIN HEARTS AND MINDS

**I**f Britain was going to win the war the Government needed public opinion on its side, with people prepared to accept a high number of casualties and years of hardship as a price worth paying.

The first challenge was to make sure there were enough men to fight.

A massive recruitment drive took place during the first two years of the conflict, with more than two million men enlisting before the introduction of conscription in 1916.

Posters were printed that made Army life look exciting.

Some told men it was their duty to join, while others even tried to make them feel guilty, saying their children would be embarrassed if their father had done nothing in the war.

Made-up stories designed to stir up emotions also appeared in the press, with German soldiers accused of bayoneting babies and gouging out the eyes of civilians.

As the war dragged into a third year, the Government was worried that people were tiring of a conflict that was costing more – in money, resources and lives – that anyone could have foreseen.

In response to fears that public unrest was near, the National War Aims Committee was set up to focus on propaganda at home and given a budget of some £10 million in today's money.

Writers were paid to pen impassioned pro-war articles for local newspapers, millions of anti-German pamphlets were produced and public rallies were organised up and down the country.

Neighbouring towns were also pitched into fund-raising battles against each other to help pay for new tanks – a technique that proved so successful that tanks were diverted away from the Western Front to help raise funds at home.

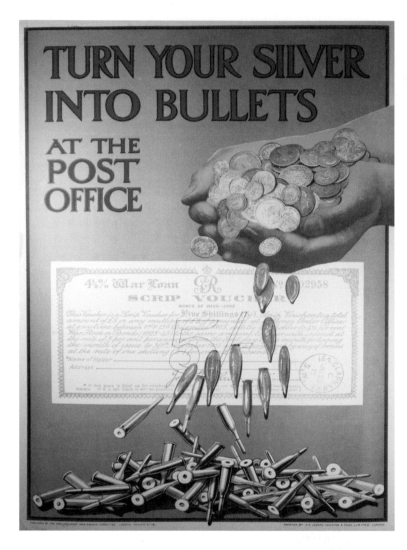

Posters were produced to encourage men to sign up to the Army, as well urge people to donate money to the war effort, top

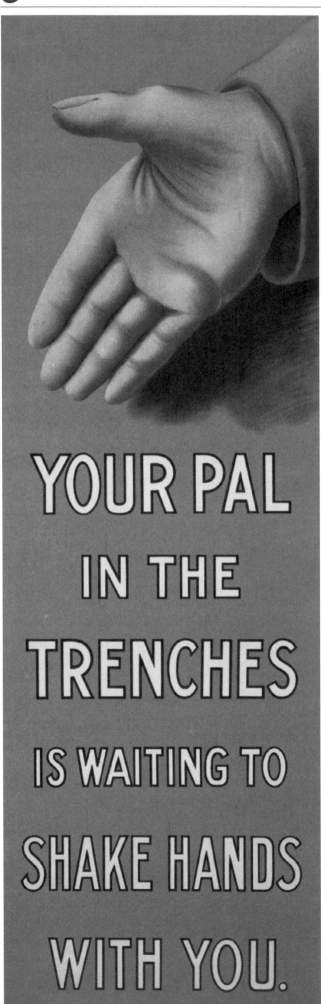

YOUR PAL
IN THE
TRENCHES
IS WAITING TO
SHAKE HANDS
WITH YOU.

JAMES WALKER (DUBLIN) LTD 30000-H.M.S.O.

Are **YOU** in this?

WOMEN OF BRITAIN
SAY—
"GO!"

# MAGIC TASTE OF FREEDOM FOR THE WOMEN STEPPING INSIDE A MAN'S WORLD

**As millions of men were shipped to the front line, the women they left behind were engaged in important and sometimes dangerous work on the home front. The need to resource the war effort and fill the void left by the men would have dramatic and long-term implications for the role of women in society...**

**"WE WERE SUCH A HAPPY BAND OF WOMEN WORKING AMONG SUCH TREACHEROUS CONDITIONS"**

**T**he terrible death of a young woman showed that it wasn't only the battlefield where lives were being put on the line.

Factory worker Grace Miles was part of the army of 'munitionettes' who helped produce the huge number of shells needed for the war effort.

It was a highly dangerous job given that bombs were likely to explode at any time and there was the constant threat of poisoning from toxic fumes.

It was overexposure to TNT that led to Grace falling ill. The 19-year-old was sent to hospital but there was nothing medics could do to save her.

"She died in terrible pain," recalled her sister, Lilian. "The continual breathing of this black powder, it sort of burnt the back of her throat away."

Before the war broke out the majority of women worked in domestic service or the textile industry.

But with a shortage of men in the workplace, women took on traditionally male roles, working in factories, transport, on farms and as police officers and firefighters.

Nearly a million women worked in munitions factories alone, for up to 12 hours a day, with the 'shell crisis' in 1915 highlighting the need for a drastic increase in the production of explosives.

The work was highly paid and, despite the danger, many women enjoyed their first real taste of freedom.

"Each day we really and truly worked as I've never seen women work like it in my life

before or since," recalled one worker known only as M Hall.

"It was just magic, we worked and we stood and we sat and we sang. If anyone had come into that factory they would never have believed it could have gone on, because we were such a happy band of women working among such treacherous conditions.

"We worked at making these little pellets, very innocent-looking little pellets, but had there been the slightest grit in those pellets it would have been 'goodbye'."

Women not only took on the work done by the millions of men sent to the trenches but their sporting activities too.

Ladies' teams, named after the munitions factories in which they worked, sprang up across the country.

The most famous of these were Dick, Kerr's Ladies FC in Preston. Founded in 1917, their matches could draw crowds of more than 50,000.

**Above**
Women at work in a munitions factory during the First World War

**Left** Preparing for another hard day's work in June 1916

The Women's Land Army also helped feed the nation by stepping into the breach left by agriculture workers who went to serve at the front. Fears of Britain being starved into submission was heightened, however, when German U-boats started attacking ships bringing in supplies from other countries.

Many women had to combine work with lengthy queues at the shops as they tried to get their hands on food which was rapidly becoming scarce.

"It was very difficult getting hold of food, especially meat," recalled Edgar Waite. "Women had to queue up very early in the morning. Somebody would say, 'Now, there's a butcher's shop up the road there, they've got some meat.'

"And they would queue up hours before the butcher's shop opened, on the off-chance of perhaps only getting a bone with a bit of meat on. They had to just accept anything that's going."

To make sure there was enough food to go around, compulsory rationing was introduced in January 1918, with the supply of sugar, meat, flour, butter, margarine and milk all strictly controlled.

It was enforced under the Defence of the Realm Act, which restricted many aspects of life on the home front, including pub opening times.

With women finding themselves with more disposable income and freed from many domestic restraints, they flocked to pubs – traditionally the preserve of men – and drank more alcohol than ever before.

This promoted moral outrage from many, with calls for the Government to take action to keep women out of bars.

Prime Minister David Lloyd George famously declared that Britain was fighting the "Germans, Austrians and drink and, as far as I can see, the greatest of these foes is drink".

Licensing laws were eventually tightened to stop factory workers turning up drunk and harming the war effort – with early morning, afternoon and earlier evening closing all introduced – although there were no measures specifically targeted at women.

> ## " WOMEN FLOCKED TO THE PUBS AND DRANK MORE ALCOHOL THAN EVER BEFORE "

The increased demands on the medical services due to the heavy casualties of war also saw a huge rise in the numbers of women involved in nursing work, with around 50,000 joining organisations such as the First Aid Nursing Yeomanry (FANY) and the Voluntary Aid Detachments (VADs).

Kept away from the dangers of direct action at the outset, by 1915 women volunteers over the age of 23 were able to serve overseas in hospitals on the Western Front, Gallipoli and Mesopotmia.

Much later on in the war the Armed Forces even began to recruit women. The Royal Navy formed the Women's Royal Navy Service (WRNS) in 1916, this was followed by the Women's Auxiliary Corps (WAACs) in 1917 and the Women's Royal Air Force (WRAF) in 1918.

These women filled administrative posts such as clerks and telephonists, worked as cooks, instructors, code experts and electricians. This freed up the men who had previously performed these jobs to join the fighting.

By the armistice, 900,000 women had served in munitions factories, 117,000 in transport jobs and 113,000 on farms. More

**Far left** People queuing for food at Smithfield Meat Market in London in 1918

**Left** Ticket collectors checking the ticket of a British soldier at London's Victoria Station

**Below left** Women working the land in 1915

**Below right** A female firefighter in uniform in 1916

The Duke of Connaught, centre, and Lord Petre, left, pay a visit to a munitions factory and see the 'munitionettes' at work producing artillery shells destined for the front

than 80,000 women had volunteered for war service, with another 100,000 serving as nurses.

But despite the contribution made by women, pay remained unequal and many were laid off as soon as male workers began trickling home from the front after hostilities ceased in November 1918.

Nevertheless, the enormous contribution made by women to the war effort helped make an unanswerable case for equal treatment, and in 1918 women were given the right to vote for the first time.

"I think that the service people pioneered the beginning of votes for women and freedom for women ," said Beatrice Browne, who served as a typist with the WRNS.

"Up until then, we were brought up in a very, very strict Victorian stilted youth. It gradually got that you were free, and when the war was over, that first war, you got more freedom.

"I know I had, I was allowed out later at home when I got back. And you got ideas, you know.

"I remember starting hockey and cricket and tennis at my office and more or less it taught you to be a leader, which I think we were."

A Gas Company employee repairs a street lamp during the First World War

# Blackouts ordered after German raids

Air raids killed more than 1,400 people in Britain during the First World War, wounding some 3,400.

Britain had never expected to be attacked at home and its defences struggled at first to cope with the onslaught from both the Zeppelin airships and German navy which had shelled coastal towns such as Scarborough, Hartlepool and Whitby.

This led to the imposition of a total 'blackout' in areas thought to be liable to air raids, meaning all but the most essential outside lighting was forbidden, while individual households and businesses were bound by law to ensure that windows and doors were heavily curtained to avoid the escape of any man-made light.

By 1916, pilots from the Royal Flying Corps and Royal Naval

These homes were damaged after being hit by a German shell in Hartlepool in December 1914

Air Service were also fighting the German raiders in the skies, helped by soldiers manning guns and searchlights.

Military targets of significance were not greatly damaged and the attacks achieved little in Britain beyond death and fury in the civilian population.

Anti-German sentiment was already high, with violent disturbances in several towns and cities gripped by 'spy fever' after the war broke out, and thousands of 'enemy aliens' were interned on the Isle of Man.

These two women are pictured learning to drive trams as they filled the posts left by men serving in the Armed Forces

# THE BATTLE AT HOME

With civilians finding themselves under attack, worries about food shortages and people working in factories across the land to ensure our troops were sufficiently well-armed, a huge battle was also being waged on the home front as Britain transformed itself into a country geared for war

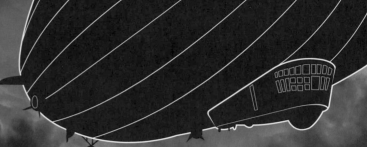

## THE WAR IN NUMBERS

### £7.4 BILLION
THE NATIONAL DEBT IN 1919, UP FROM £650M IN 1914

### 46 MILLION
POPULATION OF THE UK IN 1914

### 12 MILLION
LETTERS DELIVERED FROM BRITAIN TO THE FRONT EVERY WEEK

### £6 MILLION
HOW MUCH BRITAIN WAS SPENDING EACH DAY ON THE WAR BY 1918

### 5 MILLION
THE NUMBER OF WOMEN IN EMPLOYMENT IN JANUARY 1918, COMPARED TO 3.2 MILLION IN JULY 1914

### 30%
THE STANDARD RATE OF INCOME TAX IN 1918, COMPARED TO JUST 6% IN 1914

## "WHAT ARE TEN, TWENTY, OR THIRTY MILLIONS WHEN THE BRITISH EMPIRE IS AT STAKE? THIS IS AN ARTILLERY WAR. WE MUST HAVE EVERY GUN WE CAN LAY HANDS UPON"

DAVID LLOYD GEORGE, 1914

## INDUSTRY

The Ministry of Munitions was created in 1915 and assumed authority over all elements of war production, from appropriating raw materials to building new factories. By the end of the war, Britain had produced nearly four million rifles, a quarter of a million machine guns, 52,000 planes, 25,000 artillery pieces and more than 170 million rounds of artillery shells.

## TOTAL NUMBER OF ZEPPELIN RAIDS

# 51

More than 1,400 people died as a result of air raids in Britain during the First World War. The first Zeppelin raid took place on January 19, 1915, when two airships bombed Great Yarmouth and King's Lynn in Norfolk, killing nine people.

## STRIKES

There was a growth in labour unrest during the conflict, reaching a peak in 1917 when some 200,000 workers from 48 different towns and cities walked out in disputes mainly related to issues such as wages, food prices, war profiteering and exemption from military service. Strike leaders were imprisoned under the Defence of the Realm Act.

## INTERNMENT

There were some 60,000 Germans living in Britain at the outbreak of war. Men of fighting age, roughly 18 to 50, were interned from 1914 to 1919. They were kept in camps around the country but mainly at Douglas and Knockaloe (near Peel) in the Isle of Man, where more than 20,000 people would be held.

## NAVAL SHELLING

The first attack on British soil came on December 16, 1914, when German warships bombarded Hartlepool, Scarborough and Whitby, killing 137 people.

## POW CAMPS

When war was declared in 1914, there was no system in place on either side for dealing with prisoners of war. Camps were hastily set up, many built from scratch but existing buildings were also utilised. The early camps were found to be over-crowded, though this situation improved in Britain once makeshift camps were replaced. By the end of the conflict Britain held more than 90,000 Germans combatants prisoner.

## VOLUNTEER TRAINING CORPS

The Volunteer Training Corps was the First World War equivalent of the Home Guard, with mainly those above military age eligible to become members. Volunteers undertook a wide range of other tasks including guarding vulnerable points, munitions handling, digging anti-invasion defence lines, assisting with harvesting, firefighting and transport for wounded soldiers. In 1918, when there was an acute shortage of manpower because of the German spring offensive, 13,000 volunteers undertook three-month coast defence duties in East Anglia.

# FOOD

The Women's Land Army helped feed the nation after agriculture workers went off to fight but food became more scarce after German U-boats started attacking ships bringing in supplies from other countries. Compulsory rationing was introduced in January 1918, with the supply of sugar, meat, flour, butter, margarine and milk all strictly controlled.

# HEALTH

More than 3,000 stately homes across Britain were turned into makeshift hospitals during the war, as the country fast ran out of hospital beds when hundreds of thousands of wounded soldiers returned home from the front.
The clean country air and fine grounds were considered most helpful to rest and recuperation.

# 'COWARDS' OF WAR MADE TO FACE
# DEATH PENALTY

**For many men the horror of war proved too much. Some were driven insane while others simply ran away, but those who did flee faced brutal retribution...**

**T**he tears started to flow as the reality of war suddenly dawned on two young boys about to take part in their first attack.

No older than 17, having lied about their ages so they could fight for their country, all they wanted to do now was run for their lives.

So they fled their positions in a desperate attempt to avoid being slaughtered by German machine guns.

But both would end up being killed by British ones instead. Charged with desertion, a court martial sentenced them to death for "letting their mates down", and they were to be shot at dawn the very next day.

"The two young men were brought out to a yard and blindfolded," recalled Private William Holmes of the London Regiment.

A blindfolded man about to be executed by a firing squad of British soldiers

"The four men from my battalion who were going to shoot them, each had been given their bullets.

"And each pair were told to take one of the boys. One was to fire at the head and the other one at his heart. So the chances were that they would be killed instantly, as of course they were."

The teenagers were among 306 British soldiers shot for alleged cowardice and desertion during the First World War.

For most, their only crime was to break down amid the unspeakable horrors they had endured in the trenches.

Their condition would today be diagnosed and treated as the trauma of war but officers at the time showed no compassion for fear their comrades would have disobeyed orders and refused to go 'over the top'.

Harry Farr was among the first troops sent

Private Harry Farr was 25 when he was executed in 1916

**"**

**THE TWO YOUNG MEN WERE BROUGHT OUT TO A YARD AND BLINDFOLDED. EACH PAIR WERE TOLD TO TAKE ONE OF THE BOYS. ONE WAS TO FIRE AT THE HEAD AND THE OTHER ONE AT HIS HEART "**

shot at Carnoy, France. He refused to wear a blindfold.

Will Stones, 25, had fought courageously through the bloodshed of the Somme and in four other intense battles.

But he was executed for cowardice after he jammed his rifle across one of the narrow trenches in a quick-thinking attempt to block a rush of oncoming Germans.

He then shouted warnings to his comrades, as his senior had commanded him to, but having just seen his lieutenant shot by a group of enemy soldiers in the unexpected trench raid, he was too confused to join the counter-attack.

In the eyes of the Army authorities, this was cowardice, and the penalty was death. Despite the five men who spoke up in Will's defence, and the fact that he had been promoted above his fellow privates because of his performance as a soldier, he faced a firing squad at Arras, France, in 1917.

When Will's widow, 21-year-old Lizzie, went to collect her War Widow's Pension, she was told: "There is no pension for you. The British Army does not give pensions to cowards."

While some soldiers could not face the horror of the battlefield, others had only been following orders when they found themselves accused of desertion.

Among them was Peter Goggins, 22, who was one of seven men guarding their positions in the early hours of November 26, 1916.

Most of his fellow soldiers from 19th Durham Light Infantry had been taken off the front line after rumours the Germans were about to launch a gas attack.

As the guns fell silent, a sergeant and captain ventured into No Man's Land for a recce – but they were ambushed.

It was shortly after 2.30am when the

to France in 1915. He fought in the Battle of Neuve Chapelle, when 11,500 British soldiers died in just three days, and at Aubers Ridge, where another 11,000 troops were lost.

The ordeal left him in a French hospital with shell shock, and nurses wrote his letters home because his shaking hands could not hold a pen.

But in July 1916 he was sent back to fight at the Somme and by September he had to be dragged screaming back to the trenches.

Harry told his court martial: "I told them not to as I was sick enough as it was. The sergeant-major then grabbed my rifle and said, 'I'll blow your f***** brains out if you don't go.'"

The court martial lasted just 20 minutes and at 6am on October 18, 1916, Harry, 25, was sergeant managed to stagger back, shouting: "Run for your lives, the Huns are on top of you!"

Peter, himself a young sergeant, scrambled out of the dugout, withdrawing to a reserve trench 20 yards away – but it turned out to be a false alarm.

With the six others, he faced charges of deserting his post, and was court-martialled on Christmas Eve.

Even though the sergeant confirmed he had given the orders to retreat, Peter was executed a week later along with two others.

Another soldier wrote a moving account of the execution: "A motor ambulance arrives carrying the doomed men. Manacled and blindfolded, they are tied up to the stakes.

"Over each man's heart is placed an envelope. At the sign, the firing parties, 12 for each, align rifles on the envelopes.

"The officer holds his stick aloft and, as it falls, 36 bullets usher the souls of Kitchener's men to the great unknown."

Few soldiers wanted to be part of a firing squad.

"Everybody scuttled like a rat," remembered one after a call went out for volunteers, although one round was routinely blank so no soldier could be certain he had fired a fatal shot.

One of those who did pull the trigger was Stanley Marland, a moment which haunted him for the rest of his life.

"One of our officers, a second lieutenant, was sentenced to death and I was told to be part of the firing party," he recalled.

"At dawn one morning, eight of us were given rifles, one containing a blank cartridge. And the poor man was carried to the yard, wrapped in a blanket with a white disc on his heart.

"Six bullet holes were found in the disc and one in his throat.

"We then had to bury him and his family was told he was killed in action. He should never have been in the war, his mind was affected. In fact he was half dead when we shot him."

Rifleman Henry Williamson was at Armentieres in France when he was asked to take part in the execution of a deserter.

"He was tied to a post against a wall in his civilian clothes, and we were told to fire at a piece of white cloth pinned over his heart," he remembered.

"We didn't know what the rifles were loaded with – some were loaded with ball, others with blank.

"Then we had the order to fire and pull the triggers – we know by the recoil if it was loaded or not.

"Then the deserter's name was read out on three successive parades, as a warning."

Each soldier who was shot for cowardice or desertion during the conflict was eventually granted a posthumous pardon in 2006 following a lengthy campaign led by the families of the executed men.

They are commemorated at the National Memorial Arboretum in Alrewas, near Lichfield, Staffordshire, where a statue of a young soldier blindfolded and tied to a stake is on display.

The 10ft-high figure is modelled on 17-year-old Herbert Burden, of the Northumberland Fusiliers, who was executed for desertion in July 1915.

**Above** Peter Goggins, who was shot for cowardice despite being given an order to retreat.

**Right** The statue of Herbert Burden, who was executed for desertion in 1915, at the National Memorial Arboretum in Staffordshire

# Deserter's pals threaten to blow up war memorial

There was an explosive controversy over whether to add the name of a deserter on to a war memorial in one small Scottish town.

Black Watch soldier Private Peter Black, who was executed in September 1916, was seen by some as being unsuitable for the roll of honour.

When the local war memorial committee refused to include Peter's name on the monument in Newport-on-Tay, on the north-east coast of Fife, there was a public outcry.

A letter in the local paper pleaded: "Have these men no regard for the feelings of that boy's relations? Surely some broad-minded Christians will bestir themselves and see that this harrowing state of things is to put stop to once and for all – I am a soldier's mother."

Two of Peter's boyhood friends decided that it was time to take matters into their own hands and anonymously threatened to blow up the monument if his name was not included.

The friends, aptly named John Spark and John Squibb, went to a local quarry to steal gelignite which was then hidden in the necessary cool place, in the U-bend of Spark's parents' house.

A public meeting was then called in which more than 300 people attended – and the decision was reversed.

The memorial, with Peter's name on it, was unveiled in September 1922.

As for the gelignite, it was quietly taken back to the quarry, and the two friends were to receive no censure for their actions.

# EPIC DUEL TO DECIDE WHO RULED THE WAVES

**The naval arms race between Britain and Germany added to the tensions that ultimately led to war. Now, off the coast of Denmark, they finally clashed to determine who controlled the seas...**

**T**here was nowhere to hide as shells came raining down on Henry Allingham's ship in the middle of the North Sea.

"I'd never felt fear like it," he recalled. "None of us believed our eyes, or our luck, when they ricocheted off the bows."

The air mechanic was on board one of the 250 ships involved in an epic duel which came to be known as the Battle Of Jutland, the only full-scale naval battle of the war.

For nearly two years the British had established a ring of steel off the German coast that effectively prevented the movement of supplies into the country by sea.

**Below** HMS Queen Mary, right, pictured after being hit during the Battle of Jutland

......................................

**Above right** People desperately trying to flee a sinking ship

......................................

**Below right** Survivors from a torpedoed ship in 1918

Eager for a fight but restricted by Kaiser Wilhelm's fear of losing his precious naval weapon in battle, the German fleet was bottled up in its ports.

However, on May 31, 1916, the order finally came for the ships to leave their safe harbour and attack the British Grand Fleet, which was led by Admiral Sir John Jellicoe.

"It was about half-past three in the afternoon when we steamed towards the German fleet, six battlecruisers," recalled C Farmer, a signaller on board HMS Indefatigable.

"We closed near the enemy and a message came through that the flag was entangled round the mast, somebody must go up.

"So I took me sea boots off, climbed out

the foretop, went up the Jacob's ladder right to the very top. I unfurled the flag, and I sat on the wireless yard looking around. I could see all the German fleet; I made out roughly 40 ships. There was six of us."

The British lost several warships early on, and the signaller was aloft in the foretop of Indefatigable when it was struck.

"Within half a minute the ship turned right over and she was gone," he recalled. "I was 180 foot up and I was thrown well clear of the ship, otherwise I would have been sucked under.

"I was practically unconscious, turning over really. At last I came on top of the water. When I came up there was another fellow named Jimmy Green and we got a piece of wood, he was on one end and I was on the other end.

"A couple of minutes afterwards some shells came over and Jim was minus his head so I was left on my lonesome."

Petty Officer Ernest Francis remembered jumping into the freezing sea water after the battle cruiser Queen Mary was hit.

"I struck away from the ship as hard as I

## " I DIPPED UNDER TO AVOID BEING STRUCK AND STAYED UNDER AS LONG AS I COULD "

could and must have covered nearly 50 yards when there was a big smash," he said.

"A large piece seemed to be right above my head and acting on an impulse I dipped under to avoid being struck and stayed under as long as I could and then came on top again.

"Coming behind me I heard a rush of water, which looked very much like a surf breaking on a beach, and I realised it was the suction or backwash from the ship which had just gone. I hardly had time to fill my lungs with air when it was on me.

"I felt it was no use struggling against it, so I let myself go for a moment or two, then I struck out, but I felt it was a losing game and remarked to myself mentally, 'What's the use of struggling, you're done!' and actually eased my efforts to reach the top, when a small voice seemed to say, 'Dig out!'

"I started afresh and something bumped against me. I grasped it and afterwards found it was a large hammock; it undoubtedly pulled me to the top, more dead than alive."

More than 1,000 men had gone down with the Queen Mary, whose sinking was witnessed by Arthur Crown, a member of HMS Shannon's crew.

"I remember we could hear the firing and firing," he said. "I saw a terrific amount of smoke and fire that went up in the air.

"When it died down, there was nothing left to be seen.

"Subsequently, we were talking amongst ourselves: we reckoned that the Germans specialised in using armour-piercing shells more than we did."

Hundreds of men were also lost when HMS Invincible was sank, with Reginald Ashley among the witnesses.

"These shells were hitting the Invincible and the Indomitable and I saw the Invincible go down. Oh terrible, I didn't want to see anymore.

"She turned over with all these blokes hanging on to her. Then you could see the wakes of the torpedoes from the submarines coming towards each ship."

But the Royal Navy inflicted some serious damage of its own and the battle lasted into the night before the enemy fleet escaped to its home port under the cover of darkness.

While the British lost more men and ships – 6,094 and 14 compared to 2,551 and 11 – the Royal Navy could still claim a strategic victory.

It remained in control of the seas and the Germans never again jeopardized their High Seas Fleet by allowing it to battle the British. But that was of little consolation to the bereaved.

"We lost 75 men on our ship and we buried some of them at sea," remembered Arthur Gaskin, who was on board HMS Malaya.

"And my chum went. It brought home to me more when I saw them all laid out on the deck. I thought, 'Oh dear, oh dear, that was an experience I never want to have again'."

**Above** The First Cruiser Squadron, headed by Admiral Beatty's flagship, HMS Lion

**Right** Crews of sunken German ships being rowed to a waiting English war vessel after coming under fire from Royal Navy dreadnoughts

# BATTLE OF JUTLAND

## BRITAIN

### STRENGTH
TOTAL: 151 COMBAT SHIPS

| | |
|---|---|
| 28 | Battleships |
| 9 | Battle cruisers |
| 8 | Armoured crusiers |
| 26 | Light cruisers |
| 78 | Destroyers |
| 1 | Minelayer |
| 1 | Seaplane carrier |

### CASUALTIES AND LOSSES

| | |
|---|---|
| 6,094 | Killed |
| 674 | Wounded |
| 177 | Captured |
| 3 | Battlecruisers |
| 3 | Armoured cruisers |
| 8 | Destroyers |

## GERMANY

### STRENGTH
TOTAL: 99 COMBAT SHIPS

| | |
|---|---|
| 16 | Battleships |
| 5 | Battle cruisers |
| 6 | Pre-dreadnoughts |
| 11 | Light cruisers |
| 61 | Torpedo-boats |

### CASUALTIES AND LOSSES

| | |
|---|---|
| 2,551 | Killed |
| 507 | Wounded |
| 1 | Battlecruiser |
| 1 | Pre-dreadnought |
| 4 | Lightcruisers |
| 5 | Torpedo-boats |

Clockwise from top: HMS Hermes sunk in the Straits of Dover in October 1914; Sailors fight a fire aboard a British passenger cargo ship in the Atlantic as passengers prepare to abandon ship in March 1916; one of the ships involved in the Battle of Jutland, and crew members inside a Royal Navy submarine in 1917

The Royal Navy Cruiser HMS Glasgow which played a part in the Battle of Coronel on November 1, 1914. She also helped HMS Cornwall sink the Leipzig during the Battle of the Falkland Islands and caught the Dresden at Juan Fernandez Island, sinking her on March 14, 1915

# JOY AND DESPAIR ON THE DAY 'CRUELLEST' WAR CAME TO END

**On November 11, 1918, Germany finally accepted defeat and agreed an end to four years of bloodshed. The Armistice was signed at 5am but would not come into effect for another six hours to allow time for the message to reach the front lines. In the meantime, yet more lives would be lost...**

**P**rivate George Ellison was among the first British soldiers to be shipped to France after the outbreak of war in August 1914.

He had miraculously survived a poison gas attack and the horrific Battle of the Somme but, with just minutes of the conflict remaining, his luck finally ran out.

The 40-year-old was shot dead while scouting on the outskirts of the Belgian town of Mons, where his war had started four years earlier.

The former coal miner, who was the last British soldier to be killed in action, was among more than 10,000 casualties on the final day of the conflict.

"We were still fighting hard and losing men," recalled Hubert Trotman of the Royal Marine Light Infantry about the war's closing hours.

"We knew nothing of the proposed Armistice, we didn't know until a quarter to ten on that day.

"As we advanced on the village of Guiry a runner came up and told us that the Armistice would be signed at 11 o'clock that day. That was the first we knew about it."

The fighting continued until the moment the ceasefire came into force, as Major Keith Officer of the Australian Corps remembered.

"There was a German machine-gun unit giving our troops a lot of trouble," he said.

"They kept on firing until practically 11 o'clock. At precisely 11 o'clock an officer stepped out of their position, stood up, lifted his helmet and bowed to the British troops.

"He then fell in all his men in front of the trench and marched them off.

"I always thought that this was a wonderful display of confidence in British chivalry,

**Far left** Allied troops on a victory march through Mons on the morning of November 11, 1918, following the signing of the Armistice

**Above** Crowds celebrating peace outside Buckingham Palace

**Left** The German High Seas Fleet being escorted to Scapa Flow by a US battleship after surrendering to the Allies at the end of the war

because the temptation to fire on them must have been very great."

The terms of the Armistice included the withdrawal of German troops to behind their own borders, the exchange of prisoners, a promise of reparations and the handing over of German warships and submarines to the Allies.

With the enemy defeated, Prime Minister David Lloyd George was given a standing ovation as he entered the House of Commons to make a speech to MPs.

His voice was close to breaking as he read out the terms of the Armistice and said: "At eleven o'clock this morning came to an end the cruellest and most terrible war that has ever scourged mankind. I hope we may say that thus, this fateful morning, came to an end all wars.

"This is no time for words. Our hearts are too full of gratitude to which no tongue can give adequate expression."

Huge celebrations broke out throughout the country.

In London, Big Ben was rung for the

first time since the start of the war, while thousands of flag-wavers descended on Buckingham Palace and repeatedly shouted "we want the King!".

George V eventually emerged on the balcony, alongside the Queen and other members of the Royal Family, and he told the crowd: "With you I rejoice and thank God for the victories which the Allied arms have won, bringing hostilities to an end and peace within sight."

In the contrast to the jubilant scenes back home, there was a sombre mood among the soldiers still left standing after four years of conflict.

"It was a kind of anti-climax," recalled Corporal Clifford Lane of the Hertfordshire Regiment.

"We were too far gone, too exhausted really, to enjoy it. All we wanted to do was go back to our billets, there was no cheering, so singing.

"That day we had no alcohol at all. We simply celebrated the Armistice in silence and thankfulness that it was all over.

## "I SHOULD HAVE BEEN HAPPY. I WAS SAD. I THOUGHT OF THE SLAUGHTER, THE HARDSHIPS, THE WASTE AND THE FRIENDS I HAD LOST"

"I believe that happened quite a lot in France. It was such a sense of anti-climax. We were trained of all emotion. That's what it amounted to."

More than 16 million lives had been lost in a war which touched the lives of men, women and children in a way that no previous conflict had.

"The Armistice came, the day we had dreamed of," recalled Sergeant-Major Richard Tobin of the Royal Navy Division.

"The guns stopped, the fighting stopped. Four years of noise and bangs ended in silence.

"The killing had stopped. We were stunned. I had been out since 1914. I should have been happy. I was sad. I thought of the slaughter, the hardships, the waste and the friends I had lost."

**Above** Joyful soldiers and civilians celebrating in London

**Top right** Defeated German soldiers on the retreat

**Right** Wilhelm II, left, pictured in exile in Holland after being forced to abdicate as Germany's Kaiser in 1918

The railway coach where the Armistice was signed in France

# Did peace treaty set stage for new war?

The Armistice brought a halt to the fighting but the First World War did not officially come to an end until a peace treaty was signed the following year.

In January 1919 the leaders of 32 countries met in Paris for a conference which was dominated by the 'Big Three' of David Lloyd George, Georges Clemençeau and Woodrow Wilson, the leaders of Britain, France and America.

Wilson wanted a 'fair and lasting peace' with the armed forces of all nations reduced, while the French were hell-bent on revenge and wanted Germany to pay dearly for the war.

It looked as though the conference was going to break up without agreement until Lloyd George came up with a compromise. He persuaded Clemençeau to agree to the formation of the League of Nations – the forerunner to the United Nations – and a more lenient peace treaty that would

The signing of the Treaty of Versailles in Paris in 1919

not destroy Germany, while convincing Wilson to agree to a War Guilt Clause that would force Germany to accept responsibility for starting the conflict and pay for the cost of the damage – a bill set at £6.6 billion in 1921.

Germany also lost about 10% of its territory to neighbouring countries as well as control of its overseas colonies, while the strength of its armed forces were heavily reduced. The Germans argued the treaty was unfair but their protests were ignored and the Treaty of Versailles was signed on on June 28, 1919,

exactly five years after the killing of Archduke Franz Ferdinand.

The agreement was said to have created a climate of desperation that fostered the rise of Nazism.

New political groups and revolts formed – a young German soldier named Adolf Hitler would join one such group known as the German Workers' Party and rename it the Nazi Party. The rest, as they say, is history.

Even Lloyd George feared the terms of the treaty were too harsh, predicting: "We shall have to fight another war again in 25 years' time."

# 1914-1918
# WORLD WAR 1
## AS IT HAPPENED

The powerful front pages of the Daily Mirror told the story of the conflict like no other newspaper. From the assassination of Archduke Franz Ferdinand to the declaration of war on Germany, the Battle of the Somme and the day victory finally came, we look how the war was reported

THE DAILY MIRROR, Monday, June 29, 1914.

# Aged Austrian Emperor Loses His Nephew at an Assassin's Hand

# The Daily Mirror

### LATEST CERTIFIED CIRCULATION MORE THAN 960,000 COPIES PER DAY

No. 3,332. | Registered at the G.P.O. as a Newspaper | MONDAY, JUNE 29, 1914 | One Halfpenny.

## HEIR TO THE AUSTRIAN THRONE AND HIS WIFE SHOT DEAD IN STREET AT SERAJEVO AFTER BOMB HAD FAILED.

The Duchess of Hohenberg.      The Archduke Francis Ferdinand.

The Archduke, his wife and their family.

Another assassination in the history of the unhappy House of Hapsburg occurred yesterday, when the Archduke Francis Ferdinand, heir to the throne of Austria, and his wife, the Duchess of Hohenberg, were shot dead as they were leaving the railway station at Serajevo, the capital of Bosnia. The fatal shots were fired by an eighteen-year-old Servian student who had been banished from Bosnia. Before firing the revolver another assassin had flung a bomb into the carriage, but it failed to explode.

73

THE DAILY MIRROR Wednesday July 29 1914

# AUSTRIA DECLARES WAR ON SERVIA.

# The Daily Mirror

## LATEST CERTIFIED CIRCULATION MORE THAN 1,000,000 COPIES PER DAY

No. 3,358.    Registered at the G.P.O. as a Newspaper    WEDNESDAY, JULY 29, 1914    One Halfpenny.

## AUSTRIA-HUNGARY DECLARES WAR ON SERVIA: ARE WE ON THE EVE OF A TERRIBLE EUROPEAN CONFLICT?

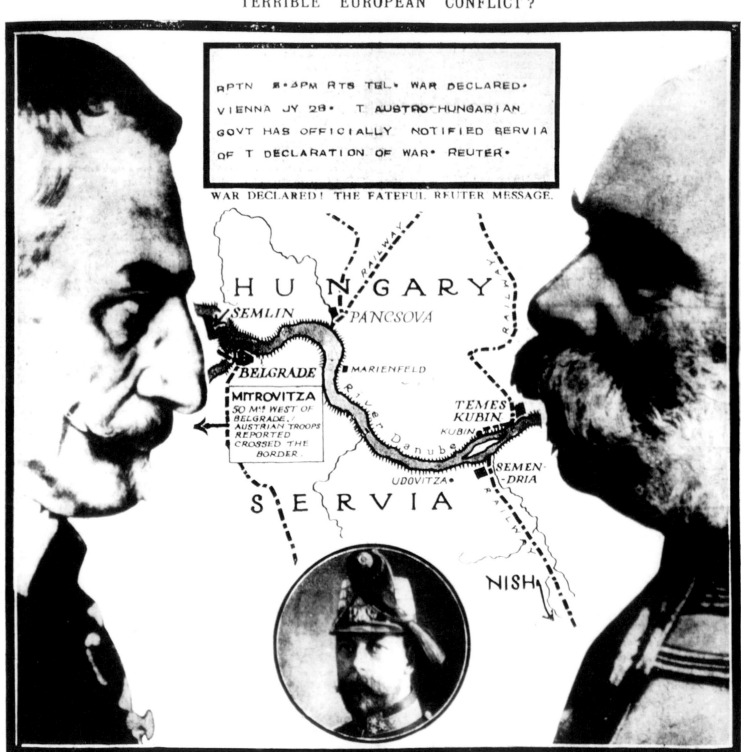

RPTN 8.4PM RTS TEL. WAR DECLARED. VIENNA JY 28. T AUSTRO-HUNGARIAN GOVT HAS OFFICIALLY NOTIFIED SERVIA OF T DECLARATION OF WAR. REUTER.

WAR DECLARED! THE FATEFUL REUTER MESSAGE.

MITROVITZA 50 M¹⁵ WEST OF BELGRADE. AUSTRIAN TROOPS REPORTED CROSSED THE BORDER.

King Peter of Servia.    How the River Danube—    King George as Austrian colonel.    —divides the two countries.    The Emperor Francis Joseph.

The war cloud which has been hanging over Europe has burst, and "Austria-Hungary finds it necessary to safeguard its rights and interests and to have recourse for this purpose to force of arms." The gravity of the news cannot easily be exaggerated, as it may involve the Great Powers of Europe in the most terrible conflict of modern times. The whole Continent is, indeed, preparing for the worst, and mobilisation is going on everywhere. The most interesting figure at the moment is Austria's aged Emperor, the murder of whose heir is the immediate cause of the war. King Peter abdicated quite recently, and the Regent is Prince Alexandre.

THE DAILY MIRROR. Monday, August 3, 1914.

# Germany Declares War on Russia and Invades France.

# The Daily Mirror

### LATEST CERTIFIED CIRCULATION MORE THAN 1,000,000 COPIES PER DAY

No. 3,362 | Registered at the G.P.O. as a Newspaper | MONDAY, AUGUST 3, 1914 | **24 PAGES.** | One Halfpenny.

## "THE SWORD IS FORCED INTO OUR HAND," SAYS THE KAISER, AND MAKES WAR ON RUSSIA AND FRANCE.

Deutschland und Österreich

Sie sollen uns nur kommen!

It is Armageddon. Germany has declared war on Russia and, it was reported yesterday, is massing troops on the French frontier. Britain is taking its holiday under a sense of appalling calamity and of impending destruction which makes one shudder to contemplate. On Saturday the Kaiser made a warlike speech, and said, "The sword is being thrust into our hand." Then the die was cast, and London learnt the dread news at supper time. The War Lord is seen wearing the uniform of the "Death's Head Hussars." The postcard, which has an enormous sale, shows a German and an Austrian soldier standing side by side. The inscription means "Let them all come."

THE DAILY MIRROR, Tuesday, August 4, 1914.

## Success of Our New Serial, "The Influence of a Girl": See page 11.

# The Daily Mirror

### LATEST CERTIFIED CIRCULATION MORE THAN 1,000,000 COPIES PER DAY

No. 3,363.    Registered at the G.P.O. as a Newspaper.    TUESDAY, AUGUST 4, 1914    One Halfpenny.

## KING GEORGE SIGNS THE ARMY MOBILISATION ORDER: THE FRENCH COAST PROTECTED BY THE BRITISH FLEET.

The thoughts of all Britishers went out to sea yesterday, for with the statement of Sir Edward Grey in Parliament, the safety and sanctity of the Empire may easily again depend upon the Navy which has given us so heroic a history. Britain's position was clearly outlined by the Foreign Secretary. France's fleet was concentrated in the Mediterranean, as an act of friendship to England. If her enemy's fleet sails down the English Channel to attack the coast of France, we cannot stand aside. Sir Edward also announced that the mobilisation of the Army is taking place, but we have not taken any engagement to send an expeditionary army abroad.

**GREAT BRITAIN DECLARES WAR ON GERMANY.**

# The Daily Mirror

LATEST CERTIFIED CIRCULATION MORE THAN 1,000,000 COPIES PER DAY

No. 3,364. | WEDNESDAY, AUGUST 5, 1914. | One Halfpenny.

## DECLARATION OF WAR BY GREAT BRITAIN AFTER UNSATIS-FACTORY REPLY TO YESTERDAY'S ULTIMATUM.

Neptune's imps. They are torpedo-boats steaming in close order to enable them to send verbal messages one to another by means of a megaphone.

Field-Marshal Sir John French. | Rear-Admiral C. E. Madden. | Admiral Sir John Jellicoe. | Field-Marshal Earl Kitchener.

Remarkable picture of a submarine rising to the surface. Are we soon to know what these unknown quantities are capable of?

There are four men—two sailors and two soldiers—to whom the Empire will turn in her hour of need. The sailors are Admiral Sir John Jellicoe (known as "the future Nelson"), who has assumed supreme command of the Home Fleets with the acting rank of Admiral, and Rear-Admiral Charles E. Madden, who has been appointed to be his Chief of Staff. The soldiers are Lord Kitchener, whose achievements are known to everyone, and Sir John French, probably the finest cavalry leader in the world, who performed brilliant feats in South Africa, "the grave of reputations."—(Bassano, Symonds, Russell and Gale and Polden.)

# 'This war has been forced upon us'

"We made every effort any Government could possibly make for peace – but this war has been forced upon us," said Prime Minister Herbert Asquith.

Speaking to the House of Commons two days after declaring war on Germany, he said the decision had been made with "utmost reluctance and with infinite regret".

Mr Asquith said great efforts had been made to secure peace but turning its back on Belgium would have "betrayed the interests of this country".

The war would bring about "unequalled suffering", he said, adding the sense of responsibility was impossible to describe, but the British were "unsheathing our sword in a just cause".

He added: "I do not believe any nation ever entered into a great controversy – and this is one of the greatest history will ever know – with a clearer conscience and a stronger conviction that it is fighting, not for aggression, not for the maintenance even of its own selfish interest, but that it is fighting in defence of principles the maintenance of which is vital to the civilization of the world."

# Germans 'cut off boys' hands' in propaganda war

Truth is often the first casualty of war – and the Government moved quickly to ensure it controlled what the media could report.

The Defence of the Realm Act, passed on August 8, 1914, imposed censorship of journalism and of letters coming home from the front line.

It stated: "No person shall by word of mouth or in writing spread reports likely to cause disaffection or alarm among any of His Majesty's forces or among the civilian population."

The press was subject to controls of reporting troop movement, numbers or any other operational information that could be exploited by the enemy.

Soldiers writing home were also not allowed to state exactly where they were, what actions they had been involved in or anything about losses or poor morale.

As a result, the nature of warfare on the Western Front was not reported during the conflict, and was not mentioned in letters that were sent from the front.

However, Britain's media barons at the time were happy to play ball and printed headlines that were designed to stir up emotions, regardless of whether they were accurate or not.

Cutting off the hands of teenage boys, gouging out the eyes of civilians and bayoneting babies were just some of the atrocities said to have been carried out by "dastardly" German soldiers.

Among the people who fell foul of the censorship rules were the Scottish anti-war activists Willie Gallacher and John Muir, who were jailed for six months and a year respectively for a critical article which appeared in the trade union journal The Worker.

THE DAILY MIRROR, Friday, August 7, 1914.

## H.M.S. AMPHION SINKS WITH 131 MEN.

# The Daily Mirror

LATEST CERTIFIED CIRCULATION MORE THAN 1,000,000 COPIES PER DAY

No. 3,366.    FRIDAY, AUGUST 7, 1914.    One Halfpenny.

### 131 MEN PERISH IN WRECK OF BRITISH CRUISER: THE SHIP WHICH SENT GERMANY'S MINE LAYER TO HER DOOM.

Lieutenant J. C. Tovey.    The ill-fated Amphion. She was launched in 1911.    Captain C. H. Fox.

The Koenigin Luise, now at the bottom of the sea.

The launch of the Lance, which sank the mine-layer.

An official statement issued by the Admiralty last night announces that H.M.S. Amphion, a cruiser of 3,440 tons, struck a German mine and sank with the loss of the paymaster and 130 men. The captain and sixteen officers and 135 men were saved. It is also stated by the Admiralty that a line of mines had probably been laid by the Koe- nigin Luise prior to her being sunk off the Dutch coast about sixty miles from Har- wich. The vessel which sent the Koenigin Luise to her doom was H.M.S. Lance, a new destroyer. Four shots sufficed to shatter her, the first taking away her bridge and the third and fourth tearing away her stern.—(Russell.)

# "SOLDIERS WRITING HOME WERE NOT ALLOWED TO STATE ANYTHING ABOUT LOSSES OR POOR MORALE"

HE DAILY MIRROR, Friday, August 21, 1914.

# THE GERMAN ARMY MAKES ITS ENTRY INTO BRUSSELS.

# The Daily Mirror

**LATEST CERTIFIED CIRCULATION MORE THAN <u>1,000,000</u> COPIES PER DAY**

No. 3,378 | Registered at the G.P.O. as a Newspaper. | FRIDAY, AUGUST 21, 1914 | One Halfpenny.

## FIRST PHOTOGRAPHS FROM THE FIRING LINE: GERMANS CAPTURE LOUVAIN ON THEIR WAY TO BRUSSELS.

Riflemen lying on the road facing the Germans at Louvain. They have made cover with brushwood and tables, and are awaiting the enemy's approach.

Belgian troops retreating into Louvain. The smoke is from houses fired by the Germans.

Helping a wounded soldier to the railway station.

Louvain, which is only fourteen miles from Brussels, has been evacuated. The Germans entered the town at night, the Belgian soldiers effecting an orderly retreat. The enemy afterwards marched on to Brussels and entered the capital yesterday. It is explained that the Belgian troops have admirably performed their duty of delaying the hostile advance and that their retirement, which has been anticipated for some days, has been dictated by the strategical situation. The Belgian army is now falling back on Antwerp. These interesting pictures are the first to reach England from the firing line.—(*Daily Mirror* photographs.)

THE DAILY MIRROR, Thursday, September 10, 1914
THE BRITISH STILL DRIVING BACK THE GERMANS.

The Daily Mirror

LATEST CERTIFIED CIRCULATION MORE THAN 1,000,000 COPIES PER DAY

No. 3,395.    Registered at the G.P.O. as a Newspaper.    THURSDAY, SEPTEMBER 10, 1914.    One Halfpenny.

SEVENTY THOUSAND INDIAN SOLDIERS TO FIGHT FOR THE EMPIRE: PRINCES GOING TO THE FRONT.

Indian lancers. Two splendid divisions of infantry and one cavalry brigade have already been despatched to Europe, while three more cavalry brigades will follow immediately.

The Maharajah Sir Pertab Singh.

The Maharajah of Jodpur, a State famous for its horses.

The Maharajah of Bikanir.

With one accord India has rallied to the defence of the Empire and given a crushing reply to the Kaiser's lying Press, which said that the great Dependency was in revolt against us. It was stated in the House of Commons yesterday that no fewer than 700 rulers of native States had offered personal service and all the resources of their territory.

It was indeed a remarkable recital, and the House, filled with grateful emotion, cheered loud and long. Seventy thousand troops will fight for the Empire, and among the Princes who will accompany the forts are the Maharajah Sir Pertab Singh and the Maharajahs of Bikanir and Jodpur.

Indian troops marching to their rest camp in Marseilles in September 1914

# "OUTPOURING OF BLOOD AND TREASURE SAVED BRITAIN IN THE OPENING MONTHS OF THE WAR"

# Empire's support for 'mother country'

When Britain declared war on Germany, support came from across the empire.

Volunteers from nations including Australia, Canada, New Zealand, India and South Africa took up arms for the "mother country". The help was invaluable as Britain's armed forces – the Royal Navy apart – were minuscule in comparison to its continental neighbours on the outbreak of war. But the imperial response outshone all hopes, with an outpouring of blood and treasure which saved Britain in the opening months and sustained it right through the conflict. The Australian Prime Minister Andrew Fisher declared: "Our duty is quite clear; to gird up our loins and remember we are Britons."

Around 2.5 million men were sent from the colonies to fight for Britain's cause during the First World War. More than 200,000 were never to return.

India was the largest single provider of troops, contributing nearly 1.3 million men. It is estimated that Canada sent some 418,000 men overseas, Australia contributed 322,000, South Africa more than 146,000, New Zealand some 124,000 and Rhodesia around 6,800. Large numbers were also provided by the West Indies and other parts of Africa and Asia.

SPFUL REUTER MESSAGE

THE DAILY MIRROR, Saturday, October 10, 1914.

## IS ANTWERP'S CATHEDRAL SHARING THE SAME FATE AS RHEIMS?

# The Daily Mirror

LATEST CERTIFIED CIRCULATION MORE THAN 1,000,000 COPIES PER DAY

No. 3,421.    Registered at the G.P.O. as a Newspaper.    SATURDAY, OCTOBER 10, 1914.    One Halfpenny.

### THE LAST TUG TO LEAVE ANTWERP: WOMEN AND CHILDREN FLY FROM THE BELEAGURED CITY.

There was a rush of refugees from Antwerp for Ostend, Holland and England, and all the boats which left the city were crowded. The pictures show women and children being put on board the last tug. Shells were bursting all the time. The citadel is still bravely defending itself against a bombardment more terrible than anything known in history. Fire, it is reported, has broken out in many places, whole streets having been reduced to ruins. It is reported that the enemy, though they pledged their word to respect all historic buildings and monuments, are shelling the cathedral, a beautiful specimen of Gothic architecture.—(*Daily Mirror* photographs.)

---

## GALLANT FRENCH TROOPS TAKE ANOTHER GERMAN TOWN

# The Daily Mirror

LATEST CERTIFIED CIRCULATION MORE THAN 1,000,000 COPIES PER DAY

THE DAILY MIRROR, Thursday, August 20, 1914.

No. 3,377.    Registered at the G.P.O. as a Newspaper.    THURSDAY, AUGUST 20, 1914.    One Halfpenny.

### THE BRITISH "TOMMIES" ENJOY THEIR VOYAGE TO FRANCE: SIR JOHN FRENCH'S ARRIVAL AT BOULOGNE.

Comrades in arms. The picture, which was taken at Boulogne, shows a Scotsman on sentry duty while the French soldier standing behind him, despite the language difficulty, making friends with another British soldier.—(*Daily Mirror* photograph.)

"Are we downhearted?" "No-o-o-o," shouts the British "Tommy." This picture was taken on board a transport, and shows how they made the cross-Channel passage.

How Sir John French came to Boulogne.

Major A. Hughes-Onslow, late 10th Hussars, who has died in France. He was with the Expeditionary force.

Sir John salutes as he steps on shore.

Thanks to our silent Navy, the English Channel was rendered absolutely safe for the passage of the transports which conveyed the British Expeditionary Force to the shores of France. There were boatloads of merry, high-spirited men who might have been going on a pleasure trip instead of to the grim business of war, and the large picture on this page shows a happy company on one of the steamers. Sir John French crossed on H.M. light cruiser Sentinel to Boulogne, whence he proceeded to Paris.

---

THE DAILY MIRROR, Thursday, September 3, 1914.

## Big P. & O. Liner as a Naval Hospital Ship: Pictures.

RUSSIA'S "Kitchener" Killed in Action Against the Germans : : Picture.

# The Daily Mirror

LATEST CERTIFIED CIRCULATION MORE THAN 1,000,000 COPIES PER DAY

REFUGEES Flock Into Paris from the Scenes of and Districts : : Pictures.

### THE BRITISH CASUALTIES: OFFICERS KILLED, WOUNDED AND MISSING.

Among the regiments whose officers have distinguished themselves in the fighting against the Germans is the Duke of Wellington's (West Riding Regiment). This group shows: (A) Captain E. V. Jenkins, D.S.O., missing; (B) Lieutenant L. E. Russell, wounded; (C) Captain C. O. Denman-Jubb, missing; (D) Captain E. R. Taylor, missing; (E) Lieutenant-Colonel J. A. C. Gibbs, wounded; (F) Major F. B. Stradford, killed; (G) Captain R. C. Carter, wounded; and (H) Lieutenant G. W. Oliphant, wounded.

Captain J. Milling (wounded).

Captain G. M. Shipway (killed).

Lieutenant H. M. Soames (killed).

Lieutenant C. E. G. Shearman (wounded).

Lieutenant W. G. S. Barker (missing).

Lieutenant-Colonel A. W. Abercrombie (missing).

Lieutenant W. A. Lieaman (wounded).

Lieutenant C. A. C. Turner (missing).

Printed and Published by THE PICTORIAL NEWSPAPER CO. (1910), Ltd., at the *Daily Mirror* Offices, 12-18, Bouverie-street, London, E.C.—Thursday, September 3, 1914.

THE DAILY MIRROR. Tuesday. November 17, 1914.

# ALLIES HURL BACK GERMANS IN BELGIUM

# The Daily Mirror

### LATEST CERTIFIED CIRCULATION MORE THAN 1,000,000 COPIES PER DAY

No. 3,453. | Registered at the G.P.O. as a Newspaper. | TUESDAY, NOVEMBER 17, 1914 | **16 PAGES.** | One Halfpenny.

## WHAT OUR HEROIC SOLDIERS HAVE TO ENDURE DAY BY DAY: ENORMOUS GERMAN FIELD GUN READY TO DEAL DEATH.

This picture gives an idea of the immense size of the weapons used in modern warfare. It shows one of the German heavy field pieces after being placed in position and men with baskets containing shells. Day after day these shells pour death into the trenches, but our heroic soldiers bear the ordeal bravely and fearlessly.

Behind this barbed entanglement a body of Austrian soldiers had taken up their position. In front of it, to prevent a charge, they had dug numbers of holes, from each of which protruded a deadly spike.

German soldier prodding a helpless and terrified woman with a bayonet during a fierce fight in a village street. The enemy evidently consider it an ordinary incident, for the picture is reproduced from a Berlin newspaper!

THE DAILY MIRROR, Thursday, December 17, 1914.

## 3 ENGLISH TOWNS SHELLED BY GERMAN NAVY

# The Daily Mirror

### CERTIFIED CIRCULATION LARGER THAN ANY OTHER DAILY NEWSPAPER IN THE WORLD

No. 3,479. | Registered at the G.P.O. as a Newspaper. | THURSDAY, DECEMBER 17, 1914 | **16 PAGES.** | One Halfpenny.

## GREAT BRITAIN BOMBARDED: GERMAN NAVY RAIDS THE COAST AND SHELLS SCARBOROUGH, WEST HARTLEPOOL AND WHITBY.

Scarborough, the " Queen of Watering Places," an unfortified town, which was bombarded by the German Navy yesterday.

Hartlepool, where the German shells made havoc yesterday. The splendid docks and the river.

Britain has been bombarded. The German Navy has at last, in part at least, dared to come out on the open seas. It has come out and raided our coast, bombarding the towns of Scarborough, West Hartlepool and Whitby with terrific shell fire yester-day morning. Fifty shells were fired into Scarborough and thirty into Whitby. Great damage has been done to property, while lives have been lost and innocent people injured. The Germans have kept their word and carried the war to Britain's shores.

Friday, January 8, 1915.

# The Daily Mirror
CERTIFIED CIRCULATION LARGER THAN ANY ● OTHER DAILY NEWSPAPER IN THE WORLD

**WHY DELAY?** THE DAILY MIRROR OVERSEAS WEEKLY EDITION contains all the Latest and Best War Pictures and News, and is therefore the Best Weekly Newspaper for your friends abroad. You can obtain it from your Newsagent for 3d. per copy. Subscription rates (prepaid), post free, to Canada for six months 10/-; elsewhere abroad 13/-. Address—Manager, "Overseas Daily Mirror," 23-29, Bouverie Street, London, E.C.

## AN HISTORIC GROUP: BRITISH AND GERMAN SOLDIERS PHOTOGRAPHED TOGETHER.

# Truce 'glimmer of humanity'

Just hours earlier both sides were desperately trying to kill each other.

But for a brief period over Christmas 1914, the bullets, bombs and bloodshed on the Western Front in the Great War gave way to a precious moment of festive peace.

All along the front line, battle-weary British and German soldiers laid down their guns and for a few hours at least – in some cases days – enjoyed some Christmas cheer.

"Just think," wrote one soldier to his family, "while you were eating turkey I was talking and shaking hands with the very men I had been trying to kill a few hours before!

"It was astounding!"

The Christmas truce of

1914 has come to represent a glimmer of humanity at the core of one of the deadliest conflicts which saw 16 million die in four years. It began when German soldiers started to sing Christmas carols. British troops responded and gradually both sets of soldiers moved out of their trenches and met in No Man's Land.

After exchanging stories and gifts, several games of football broke out.

British and German soldiers playing football on Christmas Day in 1914

The only result recorded was a 3-2 victory by the Germans, quoted in soldiers' letters from both sides.

British soldiers even wrote of cutting the hair of Germans, while others exchanged the buttons from their military jackets.

One young soldier wrote home: "They finished their carol and we thought that we ought to retaliate in some way, so we sang The First Noël, and when we finished that they all began clapping; and then they struck up another favourite of theirs, O Tannenbaum."

On some parts of the front hostilities were officially resumed on Boxing Day at 8.30am – ceremonial pistol shots marking the occasion.

THE DAILY MIRROR, Saturday, May 8, 1915.

# LUSITANIA TORPEDOED BY GERMAN PIRATE

# The Daily Mirror

### CERTIFIED CIRCULATION LARGER THAN ANY OTHER PICTURE PAPER IN THE WORLD

No. 3,600. | Registered at the G.P.O. as a Newspaper. | SATURDAY, MAY 8, 1915 | **16 PAGES** | One Halfpenny.

## GIANT CUNARDER CROWDED WITH PASSENGERS CALLOUSLY SUNK WITHOUT WARNING OFF THE IRISH COAST.

Without warning the famous Cunarder Lusitania was torpedoed off the Irish coast yesterday. She sank in eight minutes, but, it is believed, many of the passengers have been saved. The United States is seething with anger at this crime against neutral passengers, including women and children. The pirates' disregard of the lives of Americans will undoubtedly compel President Wilson to take immediate and drastic action. Amongst the passengers were many famous Britons and Americans.

THE DAILY MIRROR, Friday, May 21, 1915.

# GERMAN SPY'S CONFESSION BEFORE HANGING HIMSELF

# The Daily Mirror

### CERTIFIED CIRCULATION LARGER THAN ANY ● OTHER PICTURE PAPER IN THE WORLD

No. 3,611. | Registered at the G.P.O. as a Newspaper. | FRIDAY, MAY 21, 1915 | One Halfpenny.

## "DEVILRY, THY NAME IS GERMANY!": SOLDIERS, TRAPPED BY A GAS CLOUD, LIE UNCONSCIOUS IN THE TRENCHES.

The first effect of the gas. The men look as though utterly worn out with hard fighting; they had fallen asleep in their trench.

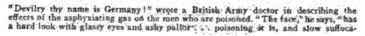

A man who had been propped up falls down again.

Both are unconscious. They had no time to escape from the fumes.

"Devilry thy name is Germany!" wrote a British Army doctor in describing the effects of the asphyxiating gas on the men who are poisoned. "The face," he says, "has a hard look with glassy eyes and ashy pallor . . . poisoning it is, and slow suffoca- tion and the tortures of the damned . . . drowning, drowning on shore, surrounded by help and friends. And never a word of complaint. They are soldiers."—(These pho- tographs are copyright in France, Canada and U.S.A.)

THE DAILY MIRROR, Thursday, July 15, 1915.

# ALLIES CAPTURE IMPORTANT POSITIONS IN DARDANELLES

# The Daily Mirror

#### CERTIFIED CIRCULATION LARGER THAN ANY OTHER PICTURE PAPER IN THE WORLD

No. 3,658. | Registered at the G.P.O. as a Newspaper. | THURSDAY, JULY 15, 1915 | One Halfpenny.

## BRITISH OFFICER LEADS AN ATTACK: A CHARGE BY THE NAVAL DIVISION ON THE GALLIPOLI PENINSULA.

Among the units which are adding such glorious pages to our history in the Dardanelles is the Royal Naval Division, and in this photograph they are seen leaping from their trench to charge the Turks. An officer is leading the men. The photograph also gives an idea of the nature of the country. Nature would seem to have designed it with a view to the defence of Constantinople, but this only adds lustre to the glorious feats of arms which have been accomplished against a brave enemy. The news from the peninsula continues good, and the report of another important success reached London yesterday. Other Dardanelles pictures appear on pages 6 and 7.

THE DAILY MIRROR, Monday, August 2, 1915.

# GREAT WAR ANNIVERSARY NUMBER

# The Daily Mirror

CERTIFIED CIRCULATION LARGER THAN ANY OTHER PICTURE PAPER IN THE WORLD

No. 3,673.   Registered at the G.P.O. as a Newspaper.   MONDAY, AUGUST 2, 1915   24 PAGES   One Halfpenny.

## WHAT THE ARMIES HAVE BEEN FACING FOR THE PAST TWELVE MONTHS.

This remarkable photograph was taken by a French dragoon while advancing against the enemy. It shows a German shell bursting between two lines while the men were charging with fixed bayonets by "leaps" of thirty yards. The picture, which is re- produced by courtesy of the Illustrated London News, was taken in a very bad light and during a heavy shower of rain. The dragoons are, of course, cavalry, but in this case are fighting on foot.

THE DAILY MIRROR, Friday, September 10, 1915.

# 106 VICTIMS OF THE ZEPPELIN RAID IN THE LONDON DISTRICT

# The Daily Mirror

## CERTIFIED CIRCULATION LARGER THAN ANY OTHER PICTURE PAPER IN THE WORLD

No. 3,707. | Registered at the G.P.O. as a Newspaper. | FRIDAY, SEPTEMBER 10, 1915 | One Halfpenny.

## WHAT LONDON LOOKS LIKE WHEN THE AIR-HUNS COME ON THEIR MISSIONS OF MURDER.

This photograph of London's night search for aerial cruisers illustrates what the great city looks like when searchlights are playing.

Following the call of the drum.

In the crowd.

One hundred and six persons were killed and injured as a result of the Zeppelin raid on the eastern counties and the London district last Wednesday. London's reply was a great new army of recruits. More than a hundred and six recruits pre-sented themselves at Trafalgar-square in response to the great appeal by Mr. Horatio Bottomley. In every part of the country men flocked to the colours. Twenty-three women and eleven children were injured by the Germans and—four soldiers.

AUSTRIA DECLARES WAR ON SERVIA.

**The Daily Mirror**

LATEST CERTIFIED CIRCULATION MORE THAN 1,000,0

# "PATRIOTISM IS NOT ENOUGH. I MUST HAVE NO HATRED OR BITTERNESS TOWARDS ANYONE"

TRAGIC STORY OF MISS CAVELL'S HEROIC DEATH

## The Daily Mirror

CERTIFIED CIRCULATION LARGER THAN ANY OTHER PICTURE PAPER IN THE WORLD

No. 3,743      FRIDAY, OCTOBER 22, 1915      One Halfpenny.

HAPPY TO DIE FOR HER COUNTRY: HOW MISS CAVELL, THE BRITISH NURSE, WAS MARTYRED BY THE GERMANS.

Mr. Brand Whitlock, the American Minister in Belgium, who left no stone unturned to prevent the infliction of the death penalty. Mr. Whitlock is well known as a novelist in the United States.

The Marquis Villalobar, the Spanish Minister in Belgium, who, with Mr. Whitlock, tried to save Miss Cavell's life.

Miss Cavell in nurse's uniform. She was accused of harbouring Allied soldiers. There was no charge of espionage.

Miss Cavell, who was known as "the Florence Nightingale of Brussels."

To-day the nation's heart will be stirred by the publication of the true story of Miss Edith Cavell, the British nurse, who was executed by the Germans. Every effort to save her was made by Mr. Brand Whitlock and the Marquis Villalobar. At the end Miss Cavell said: "I am happy to die for my country." In response to the appeals of readers, *The Daily Mirror* is organising a Cavell Memorial Fund to perpetuate this heroic woman's memory.

# Nurse 'glad to die for country'

British nurse Edith Cavell was executed by a German firing squad after helping Allied soldiers flee Belgium.

She had been in the country working as a matron at a private hospital and nurse training school but, following the occupation of Brussels, this was converted into a military hospital for soldiers of all nationalities.

She went on to actively aid the escape of soldiers under her care, helping more than 200 of them flee to neutral Holland. The 49-year-old was subsequently court-martialed, found guilty of treason and executed on October 12, 1915.

Norfolk-born Edith became known as the heroic nurse murdered by the barbarian Germans, as the British Government seized on the

propaganda advantage her death offered. On the evening before her execution, Edith was visited by an army chaplain, who she told: "Patriotism is not enough. I must have no hatred or bitterness towards anyone."

These words are inscribed on a statue erected to commemorate her near

Pictured is a naval guard of honour as Edith Cavell's coffin is brought ashore in Dover in May 1919

Trafalgar Square. When facing the firing squad, Edith said: "My soul, as I believe, is safe, and I am glad to die for my country".

Her remains were returned to Britain after the war. A state funeral was held at Westminster Abbey and she was reburied in the grounds of Norwich Cathedral.

THE DAILY MIRROR Thursday, November 4, 1915.

# NEWSAGENTS WHO SOLD OUT OF "SUNDAY PICTORIALS" LAST WEEK SHOULD REVISE THEIR ORDERS TO-DAY

# The Daily Mirror

CERTIFIED CIRCULATION LARGER THAN ANY OTHER PICTURE PAPER IN THE WORLD

No. 3,754. | Registered at the G.P.O. as a Newspaper. | THURSDAY, NOVEMBER 4, 1915 | One Halfpenny.

## THE OLD GUARD'S SALUTE: A STEADY FLOW OF RECRUITS WHICH MUST BE KEPT UP DAY BY DAY.

Two Chelsea pensioners salute the men who are going "to reap renown." They have already done their share, as their medals show.

Recruits answering their names at the Horse Guards Parade yesterday morning. All classes of men were represented.

It is the "right stuff" which is answering the call to arms, and the men are rolling up as they did at the outbreak of war. In London long lines of men are frequently to be met with marching behind the recruiting bands, and the rush at Scotland Yard and the Horse Guards Parade has been very great. The King's inspiring order of the day has undoubtedly influenced many men and shown them the way the path of duty lies.— (*Daily Mirror* photographs.)

THE DAILY MIRROR, Friday, November 12, 1915.

# STERN LAST WARNING TO ALL SINGLE MEN

# The Daily Mirror

## CERTIFIED CIRCULATION LARGER THAN ANY OTHER PICTURE PAPER IN THE WORLD

No. 3,761.    Registered at the G.P.O. as a Newspaper.    FRIDAY, NOVEMBER 12, 1915    One Halfpenny.

## THE RESPONSIBLE FIVE: NEW WAR    THE PREMIER ANNOUNCES COMMITTEE.

In the House of Commons yesterday Mr. Asquith announced that in the temporary absence of Lord Kitchener the composition of the War Committee of the Cabinet would be Mr. Balfour, Mr. McKenna, Mr. Lloyd George, Mr. Bonar Law, and the Premier. The names are given in the order in which they appear in the photograph, reading from left to right. Mr. Asquith also stated that Lord Kitchener had not tendered his resignation either to the King or to himself. A statement was issued by the Press Bureau last night in which Lord Derby, on the authority of the Prime Minister, warns "eligibles" that compulsion will be applied to them before married men are called up.

## A FEATHER IN HER CAP.    PRISONERS IN GERMANY.    SIR E. GREY'S REVELATION.

Lieutenant-Colonel Bolton and the Earl of Stair, who are among those incarcerated at Crefeld. Both officers are in the Scots Guards. The conditions obtaining at this camp, it was recently stated, have greatly improved.

### THE DRINK PROBLEM.

Adorning the Queen of Spain's hat with a feather from a "kill" at a shooting party. King Alfonso was one of the guns.

Mrs. Creighton, the widow of Bishop Creighton, who has been appointed chairman of the committee which is to inquire into the alleged excessive drinking now prevalent among certain sections of women. (Elliott and Fry.)

Sir E. Grey and Lord Haldane. Sir Edward said yesterday that he wished to resign at the same time that the Lord Chancellor retired.

# Why some men had no choice but to go off and fight

In August 1914, throngs of British men lined up to enlist in the war that many believed would be 'over by Christmas'.

Lord Kitchener, the Secretary of State for War, issued orders to expand the Army. Soldiers needed to be aged between 19 and 30, and at least 5ft 3ins tall.

More than one million men had enlisted by January 1915. However, this was not enough to keep pace with rising casualties.

By the autumn of 1915, the number of British recruits was no way near Kitchener's recommended 35,000 a week.

And while the idea of forcing men to fight went against the very core of the Liberal Party's ideology, it was recognised that a series of military disasters had also made conscription necessary.

So voluntary service was replaced with conscription in January 1916 through The Military Service Act.

This called for the enlistment of all unmarried or widowed men, without dependent children, between the ages of 18 and 41.

This was extended to married men four months later and, in 1918, the age limit was raised to 51.

Exempted were the medically unfit, clergymen, teachers and certain classes of industrial worker.

Conscientious objectors – men who objected to fighting on moral grounds – were also exempted, and were in most cases given civilian jobs or non-fighting roles at the front.

Conscription was not popular and in April 1916 more than 200,000 people demonstrated against it in Trafalgar Square.

Although many men failed to respond to the call-up, in the first year 1.1 million enlisted, and during the whole of the war conscription had raised some 2.5 million men.

---

There were no posters and no meetings in Trafalgar-square in the old days. The press gang had its own peculiar methods of filling up any vacancies which occurred,

and this picture illustrates the "send-off" of a recruit. It is by Gillray, and is entitled "The Liberty of the Subject." Gillray lived between 1757 and 1815.

In August, 1914, men struggled to enlist.

—and mounted police were necessary to regulate the crowds outside the recruiting stations.

"If young men medically fit and not indispensable to any business of national importance, or to any business conducted for the general good of the community, do not come forward voluntarily before November 30, the Government will after that date take the necessary steps to redeem the pledge made on November 2." The pledge means "other

and compulsory means would be taken before the married men were called upon to fulfil their engagement to serve." Great Britain has not always had the voluntary system. Rough-and-ready means were taken to fill up the ranks, and the press gang did not stop to listen to any objections which might be put forth.

---

# "CONSCRIPTION WAS NOT POPULAR AND IN APRIL 1916 MORE THAN 200,000 PEOPLE DEMONSTRATED AGAINST IT IN TRAFALGAR SQUARE"

Rebel prisoners being marched out of Dublin by British soldiers in May 1916

# Hundreds killed after Irish uprising

The outbreak of war delayed the introduction of Home Rule in Ireland, which was then still part of the United Kingdom.

However, most Irish people supported Britain's military action, with 200,000 of them – both Catholic and Protestant – volunteering to go into battle.

For the first couple of years of the conflict Ireland was relatively quiet as both mainstream nationalists and unionists acquiesced to keep their issues on hold. But this uneasy truce was broken with the Easter Rising of 1916, when a group of Irish republicans staged a rebellion against the British.

The rebels, led by the Irish Republican Brotherhood, seized key locations in Dublin and proclaimed an Irish republic independent of the UK on Easter Monday, April 24.

Initially, the authorities had just 400 troops to confront 1,000 insurgents. Reinforcements were speedily drafted in and within days roughly 1,600 rebels battled with up to 20,000 soldiers.

After six days of fighting, the rising was suppressed, resulting in the deaths of 450 people – most of which were civilians – and more than 2,600 injured.

Fifteen men identified as the leaders of the rebellion were executed.

THE DAILY MIRROR, Wednesday, April 26, 1916.

# REBEL ATTEMPT TO CAPTURE DUBLIN.—Official

# The Daily Mirror

CERTIFIED CIRCULATION LARGER THAN THAT OF ANY OTHER DAILY PICTURE PAPER

No. 3,902. Registered at the G.P.O. as a Newspaper.     WEDNESDAY, APRIL 26, 1916     One Halfpenny.

## ATTEMPTED RISING IN DUBLIN: MR. BIRRELL'S STATEMENT IN THE HOUSE OF COMMONS YESTERDAY.

The Post Office, Dublin.

Sir Roger Casement.

Lord Wimborne, Ireland's Lord Lieutenant.

Mr. Birrell arriving at the House yesterday.

Following upon the capture of the renegade Sir Roger Casement and the sinking of a German warship that was carrying arms and ammunition to Ireland comes the news that there has been a serious rising in the Irish capital itself. Mr. Birrell, the Chief Secretary for Ireland, announced yesterday in the House of Commons that the Dublin rioters had seized the Post Office and were in possession of some portions of the city itself. Twelve lives were lost during the riot.

---

THE DAILY MIRROR, Wednesday, August 4, 1915.

## GALLANT BRITISH ATTACK CARRIES RIDGE IN GALLIPOLI

# The Daily Mirror

CERTIFIED CIRCULATION LARGER THAN ANY OTHER PICTURE PAPER IN THE WORLD

No. 3,675. Registered at the G.P.O. as a Newspaper.     WEDNESDAY, AUGUST 4, 1915     One Halfpenny.

### WOUNDED MEN HAVE A NARROW ESCAPE IN THE DARDANELLES WHILE BEING TOWED OUT TO A HOSPITAL SHIP.

Two of the enemy's shells striking the water near some boatloads of wounded men who were being towed out to a hospital ship in the Dardanelles. They were, doubtless, chance shots, and there is no reason to believe that the Turk had any intention of firing on the wounded. Up to the present he has shown himself a clean fighter, and his taskmaster, the Hun, might well take a leaf out of his book in this respect. Another report of wanton massacres by the Germans was published yesterday.

### STRIKERS ATTACK THE STANDARD OIL WORKS IN NEW JERSEY: THREE KILLED AND 50 INJURED.

Fierce rioting took place during the strike at the Standard Oil plant at Bayonne, New Jersey, and the picture illustrates the attempt which was made to storm the works. Three persons were killed and fifty injured in the attack. The strikers were led by an Austrian named Baly, who was taught a lesson by Sheriff Kinkead, an ex-Congressman and Irishman, who eventually settled the dispute. Baly refused to allow Mr. Kinkead to address the men, so the sheriff replied by giving him a good drubbing.

---

THE DAILY MIRROR, Monday, December 13, 1915.

## 'SUNDAY PICTORIAL'S' CIRCULATION YESTERDAY, 2,014,480

# The Daily Mirror

CERTIFIED CIRCULATION LARGER THAN ANY OTHER PICTURE PAPER IN THE WORLD

No. 3,787. Registered at the G.P.O. as a Newspaper.     MONDAY, DECEMBER 13, 1915     16 PAGES.     One Halfpenny.

### ON THE LOOKOUT FOR SNIPERS: THE BRITISH TROOPS MEET THE BULGARIANS IN THE BALKANS.

On sniper duty waiting for the Bulgarian snipers to show themselves. The Bulgars, according to an Athens telegram, have suffered very heavy losses.

British lookout, lonely and cold. Compelled to retire towards the Greek frontier on account of the enemy. The Bulgarians, whose reports are boastful language, speak of severe defeats of the Anglo-

British mule transport in Serbia.

French troops, but they are not borne out by other messages. The fighting, however, has evidently been of a severe character. These pictures are by Mr. T. Grant, The Daily Mirror photographic correspondent in the Balkans.

THE DAILY MIRROR, Wednesday, June 7, 1916

# "K. OF K." AND STAFF GO DOWN IN CRUISER AT SEA—MARTYRS TO DUTY

# The Daily Mirror

### CERTIFIED CIRCULATION LARGER THAN THAT OF ANY OTHER DAILY PICTURE PAPER

| No. 3,938. | Registered at the G.P.O as a Newspaper. | WEDNESDAY, JUNE 7, 1916 | One Halfpenny. |

## LORD KITCHENER DROWNED ON HIS WAY TO RUSSIA: THE GREAT FIELD-MARSHAL ON BOARD A SUNKEN CRUISER.

The nation yesterday learnt with great grief that Lord Kitchener had been drowned. The Secretary of the Admiralty reported that H.M. cruiser Hampshire with the famous field-marshal and his staff on board had been sunk to the west of the Orkneys. Patrol vessels at once proceeded to the spot, but only some bodies and a capsized boat were found, and there is little hope of there being any survivors. The Hampshire was on her way to Russia. This is one of the latest portraits of the great soldier.

THE DAILY MIRROR, Monday, July 3, 1916.

## ALLIES' ADVANCE STILL CONTINUES: 7,000 PRISONERS

# The Daily Mirror

#### CERTIFIED CIRCULATION LARGER THAN THAT OF ANY OTHER DAILY PICTURE PAPER

No. 3,960.    Registered at the G.P.O. as a Newspaper.    MONDAY, JULY 3, 1916    One Halfpenny.

## FIRST OFFICIAL PHOTOGRAPH OF THE PREPARATIONS FOR THE GREAT BRITISH ADVANCE ON THE WESTERN FRONT.

One of our new heavy guns and crew who have assisted in preparing the way for the attack.—(Official photograph, Crown copyright reserved.)

Duke Albrecht of Württemberg.     Sir D. Haig receiving General Joffre on the eve of the attack.     The Crown Prince of Bavaria.

The great push for which we have been waiting has at last begun. On Saturday there were rejoicings in London and throughout the length and breadth of the Empire when it was learned that, as a result of the British advance, a labyrinth of German trenches | had been captured and the strongly-fortified villages of Montauban and Mametz stormed and occupied. Above are photographs of two of the leading generals in the German Army who have had to face the music of the English guns.

# PM's son was among fallen at Somme

Prime Minister Herbert Asquith did everything he could to stop his eldest son going to the front line – and his worst fears were realised when the 37-year-old was killed during the Battle of the Somme.

Oxford University graduate Raymond Asquith was set to follow his father into Parliament but the outbreak of war brought a halt to his political ambitions.

Feeling duty-bound to sign up because of his father's position, he initially signed up for the Queen's Westminster Rifles. But aware he would not see active service in this regiment, he transferred as a lieutenant into the 3rd battalion of the Grenadier Guards and went out to the Western Front in October 1915, much to his father's fury. The Prime Minister sought to use his

influence to transfer Raymond on to the general staff, and for four months he served at the general headquarters of the British Expeditionary Force, before he requested a return to active duty before the Battle of the Somme. On September 15, 1916, he led his men in an attack near Ginchy. He was shot in the chest and died while being carried back to the British lines.

THE DAILY MIRROR, Tuesday, August 22, 1916.

## BRITISH DEFEAT ATTACKS ON HIGH WOOD—BIG BALKAN BATTLE RAGING

# The Daily Mirror

### CERTIFIED CIRCULATION LARGER THAN THAT OF ANY OTHER DAILY PICTURE PAPER

No. 4,003. | Registered at the G.P.O. as a Newspaper. | TUESDAY, AUGUST 22, 1916 | One Halfpenny.

## WHEN THE POILU AND THE BOCHE ARE WITHIN SHOUTING DISTANCE OF EACH OTHER.

A small opening between the sacks of a barricade  In the foreground are some poilus, and at the back some Germans, whose heads can just be seen.

Tree trunk broken by a shell.—(Official photograph. Crown copyright reserved.)

Shell bursting on our barbed wire.—(Official photograph. Crown copyright reserved.)

At certain points of the line in the west the opposing trenches are quite a short distance from each other, and to-day we are able to publish a remarkable exclusive photograph showing French and Germans within shouting distance. The camera was put up on a stick and Fritz saw it, and being curious to see what was afoot, stuck up his head, forgetful for the moment of such things as rifle bullets. But the poilu was too sporting to take advantage of the targets, though the temptation must have been great.

# Fame and VC for first pilot to shoot down 'Zeppelin'

Lieutenant William Leefe Robinson was the first British pilot to down a 'Zeppelin' during the First World War.

Lighter than air and filled with hydrogen, Zeppelins were much feared and initially seemed invincible.

Capable of carrying up to two tonnes of bombs, they slipped over the British coast silently and at great height and proved hard to attack with conventional weapons.

On the night of September 2, 1916, 16 airships left their bases in Germany for a mass raid over England.

One of the airships, SL11, was intercepted and shot down over Tottenham by William, a member of the Royal Flying Corps.

This was seen by thousands of people who cheered and sang the national anthem as they saw the airship descend in flames. The explosion could be seen 35 miles away.

Britain's wartime leaders realised the massive propaganda potential in the shooting down of the first Zeppelin over the UK.

William had actually shot down one of the German army's wooden-frame Schütte-Lanz machines — not strictly a Zeppelin — but this technicality was lost on politicians and the public.

The news quickly made the headlines and William was awarded a Victoria Cross for his actions.

The pilot would later become a prisoner of war after his plane was shot down over France, during which time he suffered from poor health, and he died on New Year's Eve in 1918 from the effects of the Spanish flu pandemic. A memorial to him was later erected near the spot where the airship crashed.

SPLENDID BRITISH GAINS IN GREAT NEW ADVANCE

SPLENDID BRITISH GAINS IN GREAT NEW ADVANCE

# The Daily Mirror

CERTIFIED CIRCULATION LARGER THAN THAT OF ANY OTHER DAILY PICTURE PAPER

No. 4,016. Registered at the G.P.O. as a Newspaper.     WEDNESDAY, SEPTEMBER 6, 1916.     One Halfpenny.

### THE HERO OF SUNDAY MORNING: V.C. FOR THE YOUNG R.F.C. PILOT WHO DESTROYED THE ZEPPELIN.

Last night's *Gazette* announced that the King has awarded the Victoria Cross to Lieutenant William Leefe Robinson (Worcester Regiment and R.F.C.) for most conspicuous bravery. "He attacked an enemy airship under circumstances of great difficulty and danger ... attacked another airship during the flight." Tall and slim, with fair curly hair, Lieutenant Robinson is typically British in appearance. He is only twenty-one years of age and joined the R.F.C. nearly eighteen months ago, since when he has made a speciality of night flying. He can now include £3,000 promised by Lord Michelham.

# "THOUSANDS OF PEOPLE CHEERED AND SANG THE NATIONAL ANTHEM AS THEY SAW THE AIRSHIP DESCEND INTO FLAMES"

THE DAILY MIRROR, Wednesday, November 22, 1916.

# FIRST PICTURES OF THE TANKS IN ACTION

# The Daily Mirror

## CERTIFIED CIRCULATION LARGER THAN THAT OF ANY OTHER DAILY PICTURE PAPER

| No. 4,082. | Registered at the G.P.O. as a Newspaper. | WEDNESDAY, NOVEMBER 22, 1916 | One Halfpenny. |

## "HUSH, HUSH"—A TANK GOES "GALUMPHANT" INTO ACTION ON THE WESTERN FRONT.

At last! To-day we are able to publish the first photograph of one of his Majesty's land ships, which have been making such successful cruises on the sea of mud on the Somme. They are the first to be published in any British newspaper, and two others will be found on pages 6 and 7. This "juggernaut," this "Diplodocus," to give it but two of the hundred and one names which have been conferred upon it, was seen "galumphing" into action, its progress being best described in the immortal language of Lewis Carroll. The tanks have been at Flers—one "led" the men down the High-street—and many of the important battles of the great "push" in France. Before them barbed wire become as limp as macaroni, while they mow down trees and pass casually over trenches, dealing out death as they go. (Exclusive to *The Daily Mirror*.)

THE DAILY MIRROR, Wednesday, November 29, 1916.

# DAYLIGHT RAID ON LONDON—TWO ZEPPELINS DOWNED AT SEA

# The Daily Mirror

### CERTIFIED CIRCULATION LARGER THAN THAT OF ANY OTHER DAILY PICTURE PAPER

No. 4,088. | Registered at the G.P.O. as a Newspaper. | WEDNESDAY, NOVEMBER 29, 1916 | One Halfpenny.

## TWO MORE ZEPPELINS DESTROYED—SIX RAIDERS ACCOUNTED FOR IN THE LAST FIVE RAIDS.

Two more Zepps are down, but on this occasion they found their graves in the sea, both being accounted for off the coast. The honours are equally divided between the R.N.A.S. and the R.F.C., though the land gunners in one case claim a hit while an armed trawler also appears to have made excellent practice. From the Germans' point of view the raid was an utter and complete fiasco. No military damage was caused, although 100 bombs are known to have been dropped. The official account states that one woman died of shock, while five men, seven women and four children were injured. All the latest particulars of the raid will be found on another page.

## How Lloyd George rose to power at height of battle

One of the 20th century's most famous radicals, David Lloyd George was Chancellor of the Exchequer at the outbreak of war.

He became head of the new Ministry of Munitions following the 'shell crisis' of 1915, tasked with increasing the supply of artillery shells to the Western Front.

The Welshman, who was appointed War Secretary in July 1916, also supervised the transformation of the civilian economy to one completely geared towards war.

Unhappy with his conduct of the war and ambitious, Lloyd George connived with the Conservatives to oust Herbert Asquith, succeeding him as Prime Minister of the Liberal-Conservative coalition in December 1916.

His achievements in the last two years of the war included persuading the Royal Navy to introduce the convoy system where cargo ships went to sea in large groups escorted by warships. That dealt successfully with the problem of supply ships being attacked. He was also responsible for the unification of the Allied military command under French general Ferdinand Foch.

After the war, he played a major role in the Versailles peace treaty. He was the key British negotiator at the Paris Peace Conference, although he later concluded that the treaty was a failure, predicting renewed war within 25 years.

Immediately following the conference Lloyd George was awarded the Order of Merit by the King. When the coalition failed in October 1922 he was united again with the Asquithian liberals and later succeeded Asquith as Liberal party leader. With the decline of liberalism he never held office again. He was awarded an earldom shortly before his death in March 1945.

THE DAILY MIRROR, Thursday, December 7, 1916.

### END OF THE POLITICAL CRISIS—FALL OF BUKAREST

# The Daily Mirror

CERTIFIED CIRCULATION LARGER THAN THAT OF ANY OTHER DAILY PICTURE PAPER

No. 4,095.    Registered at the G.P.O. as a Newspaper.    THURSDAY, DECEMBER 7, 1916.    One Halfpenny.

### MR. LLOYD GEORGE TO BE PREMIER: WAR SECRETARY ACCEPTS OFFICE AFTER MR. BONAR LAW HAD DECLINED.

Lord Derby, who disclosed the history of the crisis yesterday.

Mr. Bonar Law, who declined the task of forming a Government.

Helping to keep our Armies well supplied with shells.

A young girl at work in a factory in the Midlands.

A new portrait of Mr. Lloyd George, who has now filled so many posts.

Filling shells with melinite. The women are protected by respirators.

Women have proved invaluable in the shipyards.

Making fuses for shells. Women do this work even better than men.

> ## "LLOYD GEORGE SUPERVISED THE TRANSFORMATION OF THE CIVILIAN ECONOMY TO ONE COMPLETELY GEARED TOWARDS WAR"

THE DAILY MIRROR, Wednesday, December 13, 1916.

# GERMANY MAKES AN OFFICIAL OFFER OF PEACE—KAISER'S ORDER

# The Daily Mirror

## CERTIFIED CIRCULATION LARGER THAN THAT OF ANY OTHER DAILY PICTURE PAPER

No. 4,100.　Registered at the G.P.O. as a Newspaper.　WEDNESDAY, DECEMBER 13, 1916　One Halfpenny.

# "I HAVE MADE AN OFFER TO THE ENEMY"—THE KAISER PROPOSES PEACE THROUGH HIS CHANCELLOR.

The Chancellor speaking at the last meeting. He indulged in an orgy of hate against England.

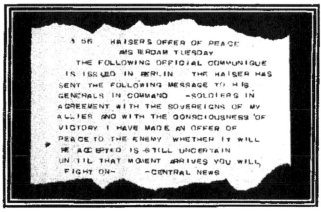

The Kaiser's message as ticked out on the Central News tape machine.

The Chancellor arriving for the last meeting of the Reichstag.

The meeting of the Reichstag, trumpeted in the Berlin Press as "of world-historic interest," took place yesterday. It was, as everyone expected, about peace, and the Chancellor announced that Germany, together with her allies, conscious of their responsibility, before God, before their own nation, and before humanity, had proposed to the hostile Powers to enter into negotiations. An official communiqué, reproduced above, in which the Kaiser said he had made an offer of peace, also reached London.

# FRANCE'S NEW GENERALISSIMO? HINTS OF DRASTIC CHANGES BY OUR ALLY'S GOVERNMENT.

General Joffre, who, it is reported, will be superseded. He will be given the rank of Marshal.

General Castelnau, General Joffre's Chief of Staff, who, it is stated, would not retain his post.

M. Painleve, to be Minister of War. If made, the appointment would be of the greatest importance.

General Robert Nivelle, who carried out the brilliant offensive at Verdun, to be the new generalissimo?

103

MORE BRITISH GAINS—NEW FOE PEACE OFFER

# The Daily Mirror

CERTIFIED CIRCULATION LARGER THAN THAT OF ANY OTHER DAILY PICTURE PAPER

No. 4,195. Registered at the G.P.O. as a Newspaper

WEDNESDAY, APRIL 4, 1917

One Penny.

U.S.A. DECLARE A STATE OF WAR WITH GERMANY—AMERICANS WHO HAVE FOUGHT AND BLED FOR THE ALLIES.

The North Atlantic fleet steaming in line of battle.

President Wilson (wearing tall-hat) at a review of troops.

Three Americans, now in the British Army, who have all been wounded. In the centre is Private O'Connor, formerly a missionary.

Marines take part in a sham battle at manœuvres. The "wounded" have fallen down.

German liners which have been interned since the beginning of the war in dock at Hoboken, New Jersey. One of the first acts expected is the seizure of the German and Austrian ships in American ports. They number eighty, including the huge liner Vaterland.

While President Wilson was delivering his great indictment of Hohenzollernism before Congress came the news that the American armed liner Aztec had been torpedoed. There were scenes of remarkable enthusiasm after the speech, the members waving handkerchiefs and flags and raising deafening cheers.

## "AMERICANS INCREASINGLY CAME TO SEE GERMANY AS THE VILLAIN"

American machine gunners are pictured in France in February 1918

# America finally steps into the fray

America entered the First World War in 1917 – after President Woodrow Wilson spent almost three years trying to stay out of the conflict.

When war was declared in Europe in 1914, the US initially adopted a policy of neutrality, though it had been an important supplier to Britain and other Allied powers.

However, the country's stance was increasingly tested.

The American public increasingly came to see Germany as the villain after news of atrocities in Belgium in 1914 and the sinking of the British passenger liner RMS Lusitania in 1915, which killed 128 Americans.

They were also outraged at the suspected German sabotage of munitions supplies in New Jersey. Despite Wilson's warning that it would not be tolerated, at the beginning of 1917 Germany decided to resume all-out submarine warfare on all merchant ships headed toward Britain. Germany also offered a military alliance to Mexico, further outraging the US just as German U-boats began sinking American ships in the North Atlantic.

Wilson asked for "a war to end all wars" that would "make the world safe for democracy" and Congress voted to declare war on April 6, 1917.

---

THE DAILY MIRROR, Thursday, April 26, 1917.

## FOOD CRISIS AND LORD DEVONPORT'S WARNING

# The Daily Mirror

CERTIFIED CIRCULATION LARGER THAN THAT OF ANY OTHER DAILY PICTURE PAPER

No. 4,213. | Registered at the G.P.O. as a Newspaper. | THURSDAY, APRIL 26, 1917. | One Penny.

## "EAT LESS OR COMPULSORY RATIONING IS INEVITABLE"—FAMOUS MEN SEND MESSAGES TO "THE DAILY MIRROR."

"A serious situation demands serious sacrifice, without which we cannot be secure," says Sir Edward Carson, the First Lord of the Admiralty, in a message to *The Daily Mirror*, in which he supports the proposal to form a National League of Food Patriots.

Within the next six or eight weeks the nation must demonstrate its readiness to eat less, or compulsory rationing will be inevitable. This plain warning was given in the House of Lords last night by Lord Devonport, the Food Controller. Food will be a decisive factor, he said.

General Sir William Robertson, Chief of the Imperial General Staff, also supports *The Daily Mirror* scheme. He thinks that the people should show their readiness to share in the sacrifices made daily by the soldiers and sailors at the front and commence in food.

### A LINK WITH THE UNKNOWN DONORS—LONDON AND NEWCASTLE BEDS.

### DRAMATIC SEA "SCRAP."

Hanging up Newcastle's shield.

Nurse and patient looking at London's coat of arms.

Beds given by cities and towns in the British Empire are to be found in the military hospitals throughout Russia. They are denoted by shields bearing the town's coat of arms, and these form a link between the donors and the wounded soldiers, who are thus able to realise how deeply their Allies have their welfare at heart. Newcastle has given twelve beds.—(*Daily Mirror* photographs.)

Commander Edward B. B. Bingham, C.B., who commanded the destroyer Broke when she rammed an enemy vessel and fought a desperate hand-to-hand conflict with her. He was in the Antarctic with the late Captain Scott.

---

THE DAILY MIRROR, Monday, October 16, 1916.

## SINGLE BRITISH COMPANY CLEARS OUT TWO GERMAN TRENCHES

# The Daily Mirror

CERTIFIED CIRCULATION LARGER THAN THAT OF ANY OTHER DAILY PICTURE PAPER

No. 4,050. | Registered at the G.P.O. as a Newspaper. | MONDAY, OCTOBER 16, 1916. | One Halfpenny.

## "GOING OVER THE TOP": A CHARGE BY THE CANADIAN TROOPS ON THE SOMME FRONT.

Fixing their bayonets in a trench—

—This done, the command is given to charge, and the men jump over the top.

This is what they had to face. The photograph shows a heavy German barrage during an attack.

---

THE DAILY MIRROR, Monday, September 25, 1916.

## HOW TERROR-STRUCK HUNS LEAPT TO DEATH FROM FLAMING ZEPP

# The Daily Mirror

CERTIFIED CIRCULATION LARGER THAN THAT OF ANY OTHER DAILY PICTURE PAPER

No. 4,032. | Registered at the G.P.O. as a Newspaper. | MONDAY, SEPTEMBER 25, 1916. | One Halfpenny.

## BETTER STILL: TWO AIR RAIDERS ARE BROUGHT DOWN IN ESSEX AND ONE OF THE CREWS CAPTURED.

A Zeppelin flying over the eastern counties at night.

A Lewis anti-aircraft gun in action.

Debris of Zeppelin brought down by the French at Brabant Le Roy.

Fourteen or fifteen airships took part in the great air raid on Great Britain on Saturday night and yesterday morning. Of these two large airships of a new pattern, and met their doom in Essex. One of them fell in flames and was destroyed, together with the occupants, but in the case of the second, the crew of twenty-two officers and men were made prisoners. London, the South-Eastern, Eastern, East Midland Counties and Lincolnshire were visited.

THE DAILY MIRROR. Monday, May 7, 1917.

# ALLIES HURL BACK GERMAN NIGHT ATTACKS

# The Daily Mirror

CERTIFIED CIRCULATION LARGER THAN THAT OF ANY OTHER DAILY PICTURE PAPER

No. 4,222. | Registered at the G.P.O. as a Newspaper. | MONDAY, MAY 7, 1917 | One Penny.

## REMARKABLE PHOTOGRAPH OF MEN CALMLY GOING ON WITH THEIR WORK WITH SHELLS BURSTING ROUND THEM.

Cyclist orderlies repairing machines under fire. A shell has burst near them and sent up a shower of mud, which looks like a volcanic eruption.—(Official photograph.)

The ruins of the beautiful Chateau of Caulincourt in the Somme.—(Official photograph.)

A large naval gun, which is helping to pepper the Boche.—(Canadian War Records.)

Included in the Huns' long list of crimes is the destruction of the Chateau of Caulincourt. Everything of beauty or historic interest is blown up by their incendiaries and in the case illustrated above the ruins were blown into the Somme, so that the British had to make a passage for the water. We continue to be successful on the western front and the enemy's attempts to re-establish himself on the lost portions of the Hindenburg line have proved futile.

THE DAILY MIRROR, Saturday, May 19, 1917.

# BRITISH ARTILLERY ON THE ITALIAN FRONT

# The Daily Mirror

## CERTIFIED CIRCULATION LARGER THAN THAT OF ANY OTHER DAILY PICTURE PAPER

No. 4,233. | Registered at the G.P.O. as a Newspaper. | SATURDAY, MAY 19, 1917 | One Penny.

## "VIVE LA FRANCE!" SHOUTS A CAPTAIN AS HIS SHIP SINKS

Leaving the French liner Sontay a few seconds before she made her final plunge. The crew showed that France's sailors possess the same indomitable spirit as her soldiers, and the captain, seeing that all his men were not off the ship, refused to don a lifebelt and remained on the bridge until the water reached it. Then he ran to the stern, which was above water and when last seen was waving his cap and shouting "Vive La France!". For other photographs see pages 6 and 7 --(Exclusive to *The Daily Mirror*.)

THE DAILY MIRROR, Monday, August 6, 1917.

# CANADIANS PUSH THEIR WAY NEARER TO LENS

# The Daily Mirror

CERTIFIED CIRCULATION LARGER THAN THAT OF ANY OTHER DAILY PICTURE PAPER

No. 4,300. | Registered at the G.P.O. as a Newspaper. | MONDAY, AUGUST 6, 1917 | One Penny.

## THREE YEARS OF FRIGHTFULNESS—LIQUID FLAME JETS

A striking photograph showing liquid flame projected from jets. This form of warfare is one of the barbarous methods first introduced by the Germans, and which the Allies have very regretfully had to adopt in self-defence. Now that we are in the fourth year of war it is opportune to point out that, besides gross brutality to civilians, the Huns have used liquid flame, gas, murdered seamen with the U boats and done a hundred and one things which are against all the laws of civilised nations.

## YESTERDAY'S WAR ANNIVERSARY SERVICE: THE KING ATTENDS AS A PRIVATE WORSHIPPER.

Admiral Sir John and Lady Jellicoe arriving.

The King leaving. With his Majesty were Princess Victoria, Princess Mary and Prince John.

To mark the commencement of the fourth year of war, an impressive but purely informal service was held at Westminster Abbey yesterday. The King was present, but he attended as a private worshipper, and no ceremonial marked his arrival or departure.

Famous sailors and soldiers, several Ministers of State and Ambassadors of the Allies were among the congregation, while there were special seats for fifty seriously-wounded soldiers. A number of fighting men from overseas were also present.

THE DAILY MIRROR, Thursday, January 17, 1918.

# 6 BIG SHIPS DOWN—LENIN'S THREAT TO RUMANIA

# The Daily Mirror

## CERTIFIED CIRCULATION LARGER THAN THAT OF ANY OTHER DAILY PICTURE PAPER

No. 4,440. | Registered at the G.P.O. as a Newspaper. | THURSDAY, JANUARY 17, 1918 | One Penny.

## RATIONS AT LAST.

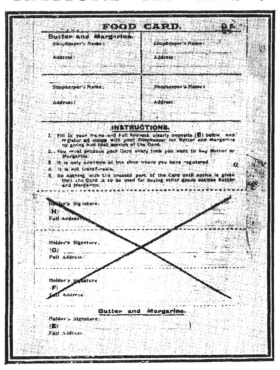

This is the official food card, which it is proposed to issue for London and the Home Counties, and will serve as a standard for the whole country.

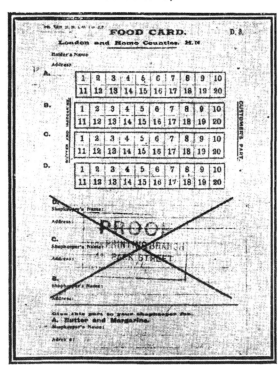

Note that there are four sections for different food commodities, and that butter and margarine are the first to be rationed. The remaining spaces will be filled in with the names of other foods that are rationed. The card will be issued to individuals and not to households. Further details on page 2.

## HOW THE GERMANS SAW THE TANKS

A remarkable photograph, taken from a German aeroplane, showing four British tanks going into action at the Cambrai battle.— (Exclusive to *The Daily Mirror*.)

## SOME LUCKY ESCAPES FROM THE YARMOUTH BOMBARDMENT.

A woman who was buried in the debris of a house. When extricated she found her mother was dead.

Rita Dyson, the nine-year-old sister of Basil Dyson, who was found during the bombardment sitting and quietly crying on the side of the bed. Shrapnel was found all over the bed in which the child had been lying.

The elder sister of Basil Dyson, the door of whose room was blown in on her bed.

This man, a bricklayer's labourer, had a miraculous escape from death. His wife was killed in her bed.

Basil Dyson, a thirteen-year-old boy, who contrived to escape, though the room was badly damaged.

109

THE DAILY MIRROR, Friday, April 5, 1918.

# NEW GERMAN ATTACK SOUTH OF THE SOMME

# The Daily Mirror

## CERTIFIED CIRCULATION LARGER THAN THAT OF ANY OTHER DAILY PICTURE PAPER

No. 4,507. | Registered at the G.P.O. as a Newspaper. | FRIDAY, APRIL 5, 1918 | One Penny.

# SECOND PHASE OF THE GREAT OFFENSIVE

British wounded coming back through the French lines.—(Official photograph.)

French cavalry with British " Tommies " waiting for the Boche.—(Official photograph.)

## PEER'S SON TO WED.

Major the Hon. Donald Forbes, M.V.O., D.S.O.

British troops and French cavalry patrol.—(Official.)

A huge British gun which helped to resist the German advance.—(Official.)

Miss Mary Doreen Lawson.

A marriage has been arranged between Major the Hon. Donald Forbes, M.V.O., D.S.O., Royal Horse Artillery, son of the late Earl of Granard, and Miss Mary Doreen Lawson.

A group of German prisoners, captured during the recent fighting—(Official photograph.)

General Mackensen, who, it is reported, with his staff and troops, is coming from Rumania to the western front.

There has been a lull in the operations on the western front, but things have begun to move once more. North of the Somme there has been no change. South of the Somme the enemy launched heavy attacks early yesterday morning on the British and French forces, and on the British front he made progress in the direction of Hamel and Vaire Wood.

THE DAILY MIRROR, Monday, April 8, 1918.

# BRITISH REPULSE SEVERAL GERMAN ATTACKS

# The Daily Mirror

### CERTIFIED CIRCULATION LARGER THAN THAT OF ANY OTHER DAILY PICTURE PAPER

No. 4,509. Registered at the G.P.O. as a Newspaper.     MONDAY, APRIL 8, 1918     One Penny.

## BANGED, BARRED AND BOLTED—THE DOOR TO PARIS

Pilots bringing in their reports.—(Official photograph.)

Americans washing their boots after a long " hike " to the lines.—(Official photograph.)

A German scout aeroplane brought down over our lines.—(Official.)

British troops passing tanks in a French village.—(Official photograph.)

The west front of the cathedral of Amiens.—(Official photograph.)

Dr. Fritz Rauserberger, who, it is stated, is the designer of the long-range gun which has been shelling Paris

Aeroplanes ready to bring in reports of enemy's position.—(Official.)

It is reported that counter-attacks carried out by our troops re-established our former positions in Aveluy Wood, and resulted in the capture of over 120 prisoners and several machine guns. The enemy again attacked opposite Albert, but was repulsed, and another attack attempted early in the night south of Hebuterne was defeated.

German prisoners from the Battle of Neuve Chapelle are pictured here passing through Handforth, Lancashire, on their way to a nearby prisoner of war camp in March 1995

# POWs 'treated better than in WW2'

More than 1.3 million prisoners of war (POW) were held in Europe in the first six months of the First World War alone.

Camps were hastily set up, many built from scratch or existing buildings were utilised.

Usually, a large unit surrendered all its men. For example, just a few weeks into the war, 92,000 Russians surrendered during the Battle of Tannenberg, and the early camps were often overcrowded.

All nations pledged to follow the Hague and Geneva Conventions on fair treatment of prisoners of war. Camps were checked by inspectors from neutral countries and the International Red Cross. As a result, the survival rate of POWs was much higher in the First World War than the second. However, allegations of cruelty and neglect were common. Stories of brutality in Allied camps were widely reported by German propaganda – to encourage their soldiers to avoid capture and instead fight to the death. Britain likewise claimed its soldiers were persecuted in German camps.

Complaints about German camps centred on brutal treatment by guards, food shortages – for which the naval blockade by Allied forces was partly responsible – the nature of work assigned to prisoners and inadequate sanitation.

The situation for prisoners was particularly bad in Russia. Large numbers were starved and many also perished from smallpox and typhus. An estimated 25% of the prisoners held by the Russians died.

THE DAILY MIRROR, Wednesday, May 29, 1918.

## GERMANS CROSS THE AISNE—TERRIFIC FIGHTING

# The Daily Mirror

CERTIFIED CIRCULATION LARGER THAN THAT OF ANY OTHER DAILY PICTURE PAPER

No. 4,553.    Registered at the G.P.O. as a Newspaper.    WEDNESDAY, MAY 29, 1918.    One Penny.

### A CONTRAST: BRITISH HUMANITY AND HUN BRUTALITY

---

## GERMANY'S ANSWER TO PRESIDENT WILSON

# The Daily Mirror

CERTIFIED CIRCULATION LARGER THAN THAT OF ANY OTHER DAILY PICTURE PAPER

No. 4,678.    TUESDAY, OCTOBER 22, 1918.    One Penny.

### FRENCH CITIZENS HAIL THEIR BRITISH LIBERATORS

---

THE DAILY MIRROR, Tuesday, October 15, 1918.

## ALLIES STRIKE A GREAT BLOW IN FLANDERS

# The Daily Mirror

CERTIFIED CIRCULATION LARGER THAN THAT OF ANY OTHER DAILY PICTURE PAPER

No. 4,672.    TUESDAY, OCTOBER 15, 1918.    One Penny.

### WHY WE CANNOT DEAL WITH HUNS EXCEPT AS CRIMINALS

THE DAILY MIRROR, Wednesday, June 26, 1918.

# ITALIAN GAINS IN ATTACK IN MOUNTAINS

# The Daily Mirror

## CERTIFIED CIRCULATION LARGER THAN THAT OF ANY OTHER DAILY PICTURE PAPER

| No. 4,577. | Registered at the G.P.O. as a Newspaper. | WEDNESDAY, JUNE 26, 1918 | One Penny. |

# RUSSIA'S EX-TSAR REPORTED MURDERED

Attired as a private soldier

As admiral of the Russian Navy

His Consort in Uhlan uniform

Blessing the Russian troops and distributing ikons.

The Royal Family in 1913—the four daughters and the Tsarevitch.

The murder is reported of the ex-Tsar Nicholas of Russia, one of the great tragic figures of world history. The Emperor of Russia fell owing to terrible misgovernment of the great Empire over which he ruled—misgovernment due to incompetent bureaucracy and sinister treachery. The Imperial Family were living at Ekaterinburg.

THE DAILY MIRROR, Friday, September 13, 1918.

## FRANCO-AMERICAN BLOW IN VERDUN SECTOR

# The Daily Mirror

### CERTIFIED CIRCULATION LARGER THAN THAT OF ANY OTHER DAILY PICTURE PAPER

No. 4,645. | Registered at the G.P.O. as a Newspaper | FRIDAY, SEPTEMBER 13, 1918 | One Penny.

## "THE END IS NOT YET—BUT THE WORST IS OVER."

The Prime Minister receives the freedom of his native city. The keynotes of the speech that he made in response are in the two phrases quoted above. *(Daily Mirror.)*

General Max von Gallwitz, who has commanded the German armies before Verdun since the German offensive in March.

Duke Albrecht of Wurtemburg commands the German troops on the Lorraine front, the scene of the Franco-American push.

Franco-Americans yesterday began the "pinching out" of the St. Mihiel salient, which has existed since 1914. Thiaucourt, which has already fallen, is only eight miles from the Lorraine frontier.

Marshal Foch, who has shown so magnificently that he knows when to stay and when to strike against the Hun hordes.

Major-General Pershing, in chief command of the American forces which are now teaching the Huns a new lesson.

Mr. Lloyd George acknowledges the cheers of the crowd.

More than one hundred tanks aided in smashing Hun lines south and west of St. Mihiel.

Manchester munition girls ready to welcome the Prime Minister.

The latest speech of Mr. Lloyd George coincided in a peculiarly effective manner with the announcement of an attack by the Allies on a new front. He spoke of the determination of the guardians of civilisation to bring the Hun beast to its knees, and a new victory on the western line answered his words.

115

THE DAILY MIRROR, Friday, November 1, 1918.

# TURKEY GOES OUT OF THE WAR—OFFICIAL

# The Daily Mirror

## CERTIFIED CIRCULATION LARGER THAN THAT OF ANY OTHER DAILY PICTURE PAPER

No. 4,687 | Registered at the G.P.O. as a Newspaper. | FRIDAY, NOVEMBER 1, 1918 | One Penny.

# TURKEY UNRESERVEDLY SURRENDERS TO THE ALLIES

Vice-Admiral Sir S. A. Gough-Calthorpe, by whom the armistice was signed at Mudros on behalf of the Allies.

Gen. Sir Edmund Allenby, whose crushing defeats of their armies in Palestine and Syria has given the finishing blow to the Turks.

many of the prisoners from time to time recovered by us from the Turks were so emaciated and weak that they were unable to stand. Here is one being brought in

General Sir Charles Townshend, the hero of the Kut siege who was released some days ago by the Turks to carry their message of surrender to Allied commanders

Sultan Mohammed VI., who is likely to be the last figurehead of any Turkish Empire. He was only a nominal ruler

Enver Pasha, who has been the bad genius of Turkey and has at last brought it to irretrievable disaster

Showing the great empire swayed by the Osmanli Sultans which has now fallen into complete dissolution

Ismail Hakki Pasha, commanding the Turkish Tigris group of armies, who has surrendered to the British.

Gen. Sir W. R. Marshall, commanding British armies in Mesopotamia, who has received the enemy's submission.

Defences of the Dardanelles, which will now be opened to the Allied Fleets.

Constantinople, now under control of Western Powers, was for centuries in Turkish hands.

Turkey is now definitely out of the war. The Turkish armies are to lay down their arms, all prisoners in the hands of the Turks are immediately to be released, and the

Allied Fleets are to be given free passage through the Dardanelles. An effective Allied occupation of Constantinople may be regarded as definitely foreshadowed.

THE DAILY MIRROR, Monday, November 4, 1918.

# PREMIER'S MESSAGE: 'AUSTRIA OUT OF THE WAR'

# The Daily Mirror

## CERTIFIED CIRCULATION LARGER THAN THAT OF ANY OTHER DAILY PICTURE PAPER

No. 4,689. | Registered at the G.P.O. as a Newspaper. | MONDAY, NOVEMBER 4, 1918 | One Penny.

# WHAT IS LEFT OF AUSTRIA SUBMITS TO THE ALLIES

General Treat, commanding the American contingent operating against Austria.

General the Earl of Cavan, commanding British forces operating against Austria.

General Diaz, Commander-in-Chief of Allied Forces operating against Austria.

General Grazaini, commanding French forces operating against Austria.

Baron von Burian, one of the architects of the downfall of the Austro-Hungarian Empire. He was used as a "peace-dove," but could not act the part.

Count Czernin, one of the most powerful supporters of Austro-Hungarian Imperial sin, who now has an opportunity of witnessing the result of his work.

The Austrian armistice creates a new peril for Germany, for it exposes her southern flank to an Allied attack. Defensive preparations are being feverishly prepared in Bavaria—and the Italians are advancing in the Trentino, which is south of the Tyrol.

Gen. Boroevic, in command of one of the principal Austrian armies, whose forces were put entirely out of action by the swift Italian advance.

The Archduke Joseph, who made a last attempt to maintain Hapsburg rule in Budapest, but was swept away by the torrent of popular feeling.

A recent portrait of the Empress Zita with one of her children.

The late Emperor Francis Joseph, who died too soon to see the ruin to which he led both his dynasty and his subjects. He is happier than those who survive him.

The ill-fated Archduke Franz Ferdinand, whose assassination in Serajevo was made the pretext for the diplomatic quarrel that led to the great war.

The Emperor Karl of the Austria that was with the little Crown Prince who will never succeed

An armistice has been signed by General Diaz, Commander-in-Chief of the Italian armies, by which hostilities with the military forces of Austria-Hungary cease from three o'clock to-day. Italian troops and naval forces have already landed at Trieste, Austria's principal port.

117

THE DAILY MIRROR, Monday, November 11, 1918.

# ARRIVAL OF ARMISTICE COURIER AT SPA

# The Daily Mirror

## CERTIFIED CIRCULATION LARGER THAN THAT OF ANY OTHER DAILY PICTURE PAPER

No. 4,695. | Registered at the G.P.O. as a Newspaper. | MONDAY, NOVEMBER 11, 1918 | One Penny.

# DEMOCRACY TRIUMPHS OVER LAST OF THE AUTOCRATS

The Kaiser and his son need not bid each other good-bye. They are both going the same way.

The crowd in the Mall awaits news of the enemy answer to Allies' armistice proposal amid the thickly-ranked guns captured by the British in the final battles on the western front.—(Daily Mirror photograph.)

## THEY HAVE AT LAST MADE THE WORLD SAFE FOR DEMOCRACY.

Herr Ballin, the famous director of German steamship companies and other commercial enterprises, a great friend of the Kaiser, whose death is reported.

Dr. Woodrow Wilson, President of the U.S.A., who has summed up the war and peace aims of the Allies in a series of unforgettable State documents. He would not parley with Hun militarism.

Mr. David Lloyd George, who has been Britain's trusted man at the helm through hard trials to complete victory. To him the nation has turned for the solution of all its war problems.

M. Clemenceau, the French Premier, whose energy, enthusiasm and determination have been vital forces in France. He was the embodiment of the national "will to victory."

Herr Ebert, the Socialist deputy, who is to become Chancellor in Germany as soon as present Chancellor has dealt with questions relating to Kaiser's abdication.

Herr Krupp von Bohlen, who married the heiress of the famous organiser and chief proprietor of the vast works at Essen. Said to be arrested by the revolutionaries.

The Kaiser surrounded by officers of the Imperial U-boat Service, executors of some of his most abominable crimes. It is reported some of these officers have been attacked by the mob at Hamburg.

Frau Krupp von Bohlen, whose inherited fortune and interest in the Krupp works made her one of the richest women in the world, reported to be arrested with her husband.

The renunciation of the German throne by the Kaiser and his son, the Crown Prince, marks the final disappearance of military autocracy from the affairs of nations. The great defenders of the rights of the peoples as against the privileges of the rulers have saved civilisation from the scientifically-armed barbarism which threatened to destroy it.

THE DAILY MIRROR, Tuesday, November 12, 1918.

# ALLIES' DRASTIC ARMISTICE TERMS TO HUNS

# The Daily Mirror

### CERTIFIED CIRCULATION LARGER THAN THAT OF ANY OTHER DAILY PICTURE PAPER

No. 4,696.    Registered at the G.P.O. as a Newspaper.    TUESDAY, NOVEMBER 12, 1918    One Penny.

# HOW LONDON HAILED THE END OF WAR

The King and Queen appeared on the balcony at Buckingham Palace to acknowledge the cheers of the crowd that gathered to congratulate their Majesties on the victory.

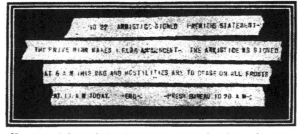

There never again will be such news for the Mercuries of the streets to cry.—(*Daily Mirror.*)

How news of the armistice signature came over the wire to the newspaper offices. A facsimile of it as automatically printed on the tape machine. The cheers which greeted it were the first to be raised.

Goddesses in the car, accompanied by a man of war, celebrate the occasion.—(*Daily Mirror.*)

Nothing gave greater satisfaction to all of us than the news that the cessation of hostilities found the British armies once more in possession of Mons, where the immortal

A historic message as it came over the wire. It is dramatic that the last British war communiqué should proclaim our forces at Mons.

"Contemptibles" first taught the Huns what British valour and steadfastness could do. They left the town as defenders of a forlorn hope; they re-entered it conquerors indeed.

119

# THE UNSEEN WAR

Daily Mirror photographers stood alongside our soldiers in the trenches, risking their lives to record events as they unfolded on the front line, and the images they captured provide a fascinating insight into the First World War

Russian troops take up positions during their battle against the Austro-Hungarian army on the Eastern Front

Tins of corned beef being handed over to a group of Royal Marines near Ostend, Belgium, in 1914

**Above** Russian machine gunners take up their position before the Battle of Lemberg in September 1914

**Left** Russian leader Tsar Nicholas II looking through a periscope at the enemy position on the front line of the Eastern Front

**Above** Three generations of refugees arrive in Brussels with the few belongings they could save before fleeing their homes

**Right** Refugees heading to the quay at Antwerp to catch one of the boats leaving the city. They came on foot, in taxis and on carts, and carried what possessions they were able to bring with them

Refugees fleeing the advancing German army are seen here in Brussels on August 10, 1914

Marines from the British Naval Brigade cooking
lunch near Antwerp in October 1914

# Mirror photographers were 'true pioneers'

Fergus McKenna, of Mirrorpix, led the huge task to unearth the Mirror's vast collection of First World War images.

Explaining the role the newspaper's photographers played in bringing home the brutal reality of war, he said: "The Mirror, along with other British newspapers, played a key role in reporting the events of 1914-1918, but the Mirror stands out almost uniquely as a photography-led daily paper.

"Our journalists were able to show an eager readership back home what was happening and what this modern warfare actually looked like on the front lines.

"However, even we were surprised when we started to research our photographic archives and uncovered such a wealth of unique first-hand First World War photography.

"Our team of archivists spent weeks researching through file after file of glass negatives and prints to piece together an astonishing picture of the war, told from the very personal perspective of our own Mirror photographers.

"The content of the pictures themselves are a rare treasure. From epic images of brave men going 'over the top', probably for the first and last time in their lives, to arguably more mundane but somehow more engaging pictures of soldiers sharing a brew of tea with their comrades and companions behind the lines.

"The Mirror photographers who documented the conflict of 1914-1918 were true pioneers. Many of them had cut their teeth in conflicts across North Africa and the Balkans in the build up to the First World War. But even so, none of them can truly have been aware of the horrors they were to face on the Western Front and beyond.

"To be there, carrying cumbersome fragile equipment, surrounded by all of that death and destruction of humanity makes them heroes in my eyes. It is an enormous privilege to be able to hold their original negatives, just as it is to share the images with our readers today."

**Right** A British Royal Marine seen here digging in a machine gun emplacement close to the Belgium port of Ostend

**Below** Before occupying Brussels, the Germans took Louvain – the key to the capital. Though hopelessly outnumbered, the Belgians resisted the advance with desperate courage, enabling the main army to fall back towards Antwerp. This picture shows Belgian troops waiting for the German advance behind a barricade on the road to Louvain

**Left** Belgian artillery, which assisted the forts during the siege of Antwerp, is seen here returning fire, hidden behind trees to conceal its position

**Right** Earthwork defences and bomb-proof shelters being built by the Belgians and the British Naval Brigade as the last line of defence on a road near Antwerp

This picture was taken just after the fall of Lier, 15 miles from Antwerp, and shows Royal Marines who, having blown up the bridge across the River Nethe, are pulling down anything that could afford the enemy cover. The houses overlooking the river were destroyed after being used by German snipers

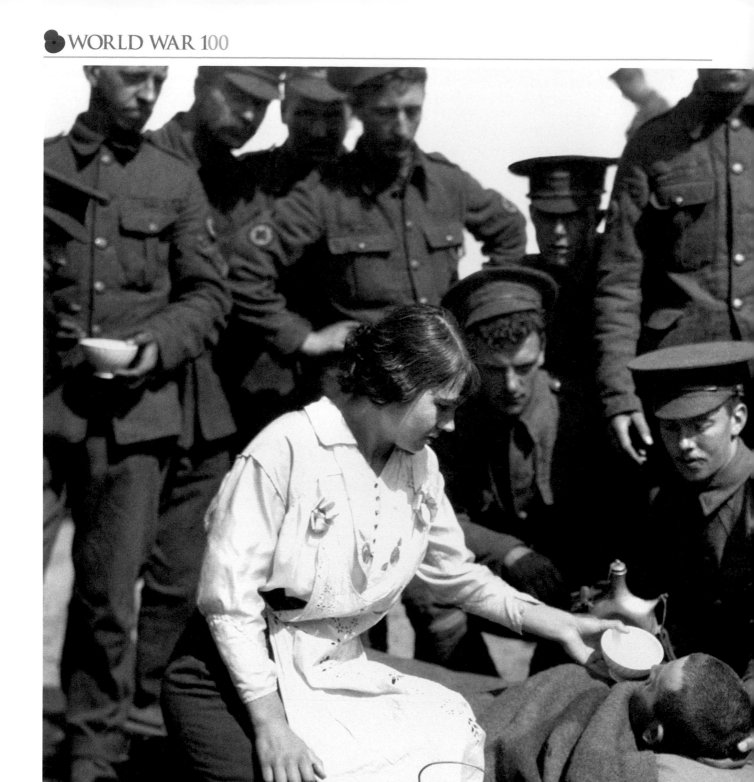

Civilians and members of the Royal Army
Medical Corps distributing refreshments to
wounded British soldiers in France

Belgian soldiers digging trenches and setting up machine guns near the town of Auderghem in September 1914

A priest with one of the youngest of the 300 Belgian refugees aboard a cross-channel ferry bringing them to Britain on September 27, 1914

**Right**
Scouts at the head of the Russian advance into the Austro-Hungarian empire

**Below**
A Belgian army armoured car near Termonde in September 1914

**Opposite**
A Royal Army Service Corps soldier in France cooks a hot meal on a makeshift field kitchen. In the background, hanging from a tree, are cooking utensils and some washed clothes

The unsung heroes of the British Army during the war, members of the Army Service Corps operated the transport, provided the food, equipment and ammunition. These men are pictured resting after a day of hard toil on October 14, 1914

Soldiers from the British Expeditionary Force receive gifts from women at Southampton in 1914

**Left** For a few brief hours, members of the British Cavalry enjoy a rest in a French stubble field, behind the cover of a protecting coppice

British volunteers for the French Foreign Legion marching through the streets of Paris in September 1914

**Right**
The Crown Prince of Germany reviews soldiers at his headquarters in October 1914

**Below**
Recruits being trained on how to manoeuvre large artillery pieces

**Opposite**
A resident of Senlis, a town destroyed by the Germans, returns to what remains of her home with her children, October 1914

Journalists talk to a Boy Scout about the German encirclement of Antwerp in October 1914

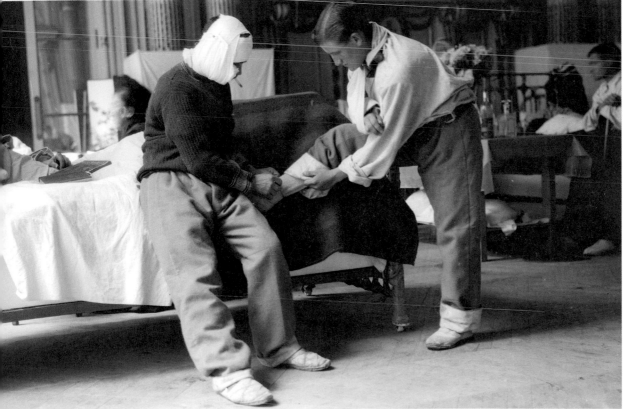

**Above** B Squadron of the South Yorkshire Regiment preparing for Sunday dinner in 1914

**Left** Many wounded British soldiers were taken to the British Women's Hospital in Paris. These patients were pictured in October 1914

Members of the Army Service Corps carry out repairs in France, with the
power for their mobile workshop supplied by motor car engines

German soldiers stop for a water break in August 1914

Refugees from the advancing German army are pictured here on the road to Brussels

**Right** A group of Scottish prisoners of war under guard at a camp near Berlin. When this image was published in the Daily Mirror on September 19, 1914, the families of many of the men shown were relieved as their loved ones had been listed as 'missing in action'

A wounded British soldier waiting for the Red Cross and a train home in time for the first Christmas of the war

A woman weeps at the roadside beside her worldly treasures in Antwerp following the German invasion of Belgium

**Below** British troops asleep in Boulogne, having just arrived to join their French and Belgian allies

A medical orderly holding a bird donated to a hospital train which carried casualties from the front line back to Saint-Nazaire

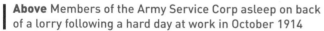

**Above** Members of the Army Service Corp asleep on back of a lorry following a hard day at work in October 1914

This photograph was taken by a wounded Royal Scots Fusiliers soldier. His comrades are seen taking cover in front of a German trench they have just captured

**Left** British prisoners of war digging trenches under the supervision of German guards in France

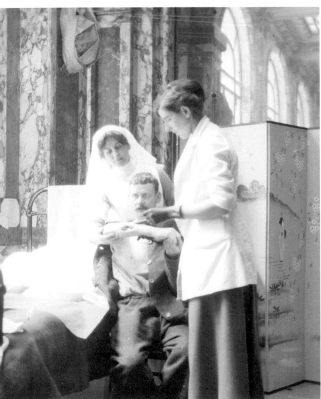

A wounded soldier is treated at the British Women's Hospital in Paris

The destruction at Louvain, Belgium, following five days of German bombardment

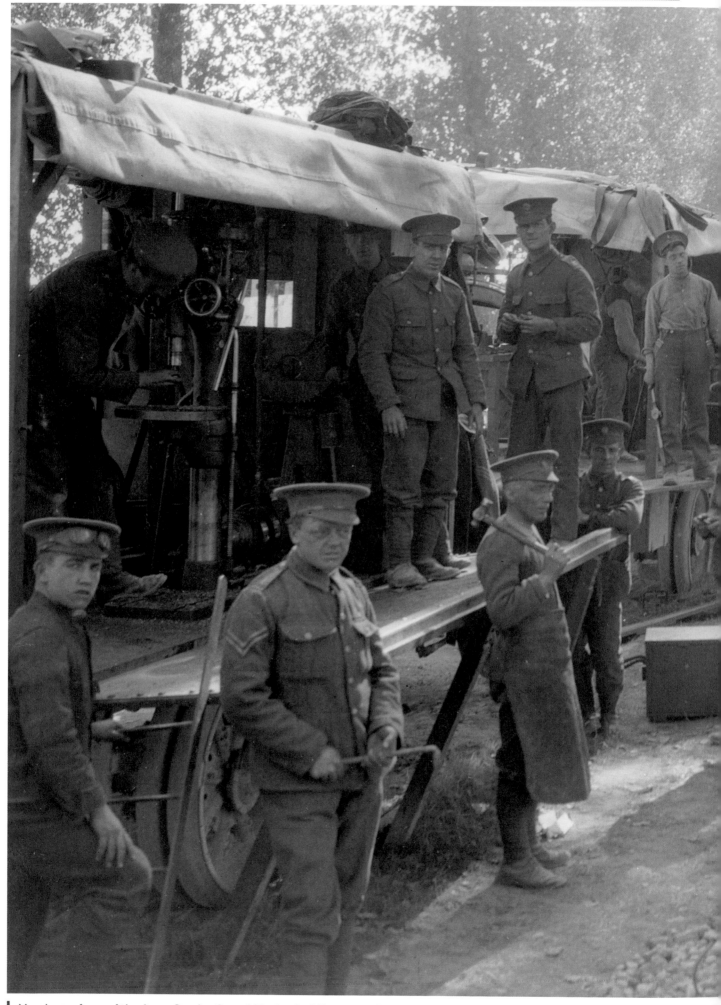
Members of one of the Army Service Corps' Mechanical Transport Companies at work in northern France in October 1914

**Right** The bodies of Belgian troops killed by shrapnel lay in a trench as their colleagues try to stem the German advance across Belgium

**Below** The Crown Prince of Germany reviewing troops at the beginning of the war

**Above** Soldiers from the 10th Worcesters are seen here bringing in German prisoners captured during the attack on La Boisselle at the beginning of the Battle of the Somme on July 3, 1916

**Right** Canadian troops sit in their foxholes manning their machine guns in 1915

Austrian troops defending a mountain outpost in December 1915 during one of the Battles of the Isonzo, which were fought between the Austro-Hungarian and Italian armies along the Isonzo River on the Italian Front

**Above** A French army dispatch dog jumps over a soldier in the trenches as it leaves with a message tied to his collar

**Right** British troops looking out for snipers in December 1915

**Above** British soldiers christened their base in
France 'Hotel De Ritz' in 1916

**Left** Irish 10th Division
troops wearing gas
masks in the trenches
in the Struma River
valley, close to
Salonika, in 1916

**Above** One of the first
victims of a poison
gas attack lays dead
during the Second
Battle of Ypres in
April 1915

ANZAC troops are pictured using a periscope to observe the movement of Turkish troops during the Battle of Gallipoli. Right, Royal Navy Division troops launching a charge during the ill-fated campaign

# Churchill's disastrous Gallipoli campaign

The Battle of Gallipoli took place on the Turkish peninsula from April 1915 to January 1916.

The campaign was intended to allow Allied ships to pass through the Dardanelles and capture Constantinople (now Istanbul).

By capturing Constantinople, the British hoped to link up with the Russians, knock Turkey out of the war and possibly persuade the Balkan states to join the Allies.

It was also believed that creating another front would force the Germans to split their army still further, leaving their lines weaker in the west and east.

But the campaign, the brainchild of Winston Churchill, turned out to be a disaster for the Allies.

British troops landed on the southern tip of the Gallipoli peninsula at Cape Helles on April 25, with Australian and New Zealand (ANZAC) troops landing further north at Gaba Tepe.

A navigational error meant the ANZAC troops who undertook

Australian troops charging a Turkish trench in December 1915

the Gaba Tepe landing were put ashore in the wrong place. Of the five separate landings at Cape Helles, three were largely unopposed but the other two, at V Beach and W Beach, witnessed heavy fighting.

Of the 950 men from the Lancashire Fusiliers who landed at W Beach, 254 were killed and a further 283 wounded in securing a foothold on the peninsula.

Far from providing a rapid

military victory, the Gallipoli campaign quickly turned into another war of attrition, with its own system of trenches and stubborn defensive lines.

More than 20,000 British soldiers had been killed by the time an evacuation was ordered after eight months of intense fighting. The campaign's failure prompted the resignation of Churchill as the First Lord of the Admiralty.

**Above** Royal Marines on guard in the Dardanelles in June 1915

**Right** Australian engineers build a bridge over a river near the pyramids in Egypt, which was declared a British protectorate and put under martial law following the outbreak of war

**Above left**
Turkish troops watch British soldiers from a troopship in the sea of Marmora

**Above**
A French officer visits the grave of Victoria Cross winner Charles Doughty-Wylie, who was killed during the Battle of Gallipoli

**Left**
A British officer leads a Turkish prisoner of war

**Above** War
Secretary Lord
Kitchener,
second right,
in December
1915 on a
tour of the
trenches in the
Dardanelles
with General
John Maxwell,
second
left. The
commanders
are within
30 yards of
the Turkish
trenches

**Right** British
artillerymen
manning a gun
mounted on a
flatbed railway
truck

**Above** A camouflaged Turkish sniper photographed immediately after capture in 1915

**Right** A French Red Cross dog finds a wounded soldier in January 1918

German prisoners help to carry wounded British soldiers back to their trenches following an attack on German units holding Ginchy during the Battle of the Somme

# BAND OF BROTHERS

PERSONAL STORIES

BEECHEY BROTHERS

**Eight men from one family went off to fight in the First World War but only three came home. The letters they wrote to their mother help to tell their harrowing story...**

**L**ike the mother of every serving soldier, Amy Beechey dreaded a knock on the door and the telegram or letter she knew would break her heart.

But it was a grief-stricken experience she went through five times as the First World War ripped her family apart.

All her eight sons – Barnard, Charles, Leonard, Christopher, Frank, Eric, Harold and Sam – went off to fight in the conflict but only three came home.

Already forced to raise her 14 children alone after the death of her clergyman husband in 1912, she kept every letter her sons sent her as she prayed for their safe return.

Those letters – stored in an attic for many years and passed down the generations – provide a vivid picture of the conflict as seen through the eyes of the brothers.

**Left to right**
Barnard, Charles, Frank, Harold and Len Beechey, the five brothers who paid the ultimate price after going off to fight for their country

Barnard Beechey was a schoolmaster and the eldest at 38. He joined the 2nd Battalion of the Lincolnshire Regiment as a private and was the first son to die.

Just a few days before he was killed in the Battle of Loos in France in September 1915, he wrote: "I really am all right and don't mind the life, only we all wish the thing was over."

Frank Beechey, also a teacher, was the next to give his life for his country. His legs were torn off by a Somme shell in November 1916.

Frank, 30 when he died, had lain in No Man's Land under enemy fire from dawn until dusk before an army doctor risked his life to crawl out and administer morphine.

Two days after getting official notice of his death Amy received a card from Frank that read: "Wounded... but going on well."

Amy fired off a telegram to the War Office asking if her son really had died. The brief, devastating reply – "regret there is no reason to doubt" – confirmed her worst fears.

Harold Beechey was perhaps the most tragic of the brothers. Having fought Turks and dysentery at Gallipoli, he survived the Somme with a wound that took him back to England.

He wrote home: "Very lucky, nice round shrapnel through arm and chest, but did not penetrate ribs. Feel I could take it out myself with a knife."

But there was little sympathy for the injured or battle-weary in Kitchener's army

> **"THE LAST THREE YEARS SEEM SO AWFUL TO US AFTER THE 20 WE SPENT IN PEACE AND ENJOYMENT"**

and he was patched up and sent back to fight again. He wrote bitterly to his mum: "To deny a fellow the right of a final leave seems to me to be miserable spitefulness on their part."

Harold had returned to the Somme after his convalescence. He had hoped to be granted the home leave he was due but this was denied. Harold would never see his beloved mother again.

On April 10, 1917, he was killed by a shell blast at Arras, aged 26, and has no known grave.

The Australian Red Cross reassured her that Harold had died quickly. She wrote back: "I am thankful he did not suffer long. This is the third of my eight sons (all in the Army) who has lost his life in France … poor boy."

Amy's next two sons, Charles and Leonard Beechey were reluctant soldiers. Char, as he was known, stayed on as a schoolmaster while his brothers rushed to join up.

Handed a telegram about a brother killed in action, he read it, tucked it into his pocket – and continued taking a maths class. After giving in to pressure to join the war, he wrote: "These last three years seem so awful to us after the 20 we spent in such peace and enjoyment, so let me now hope that we have had our share of the losses although we are taking more than our share of the dangers."

In the end, those dangers overwhelmed him. A harrowing letter from Staff Officer HM Peacock, dated on the day Charles, 39, died of a bullet wound in East Africa in October 1917, read: "I am writing you a few lines at the request of your son who is lying here with a very serious wound received in action. I am sorry to say that the doctor can give little hope and I think your son himself realises this – he is bearing himself bravely and facing the situation like a true Britisher."

His brother Leonard, a quiet, romantic boy, had worked as a railway clerk but wrote movingly as he sat amid the desolation of war.

Recalling sunset walks across Hampstead Heath with his wife Annie, he wrote: "I think in autumn there are more beautiful sunsets, but I cannot rid myself of the thought that winter lurks behind them."

Leonard died, aged 36, in December 1917 in the battle of Cambrai, his last words written in spidery handwriting from his deathbed at a French hospital were: "My darling mother, don't feel like doing much yet. Lots of love, Len."

There is a plaque commemorating the five boys in Friesthorpe, Lincolnshire, where they grew up. But it is the letters that help us to remember more vividly an ordinary family that suffered such extraordinary loss for their country.

Author Michael Walsh used the letters, now in the hands of the Museum of Lincolnshire Life after being donated by Amy's granddaughter Joey Warren, to piece together the family's story for his book *Brothers in War.*

He says: "There wasn't a family in the land that wasn't affected by the war – who hadn't lost a husband, brother, father or cousin.

"But Mrs Beechey seemed to have suffered more than her fair share."

> **THERE WASN'T A FAMILY IN THE LAND THAT WASN'T AFFECTED BY THE WAR. BUT MRS BEECHEY SEEMED TO HAVE SUFFERED MORE THAN HER FAIR SHARE**

**Below left** Amy Beechey, who lost five sons in the war

**Below** West Beach, Suvla Point, shortly before the evacuation of Gallipoli in December 1915

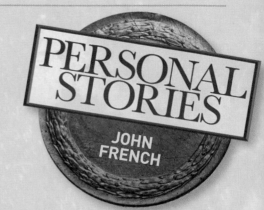

PERSONAL STORIES
JOHN FRENCH

# 'THERE WON'T BE MANY OF US LEFT AT THIS RATE...'

John French was just 23 when he left the tin mines of Cornwall for an even deadlier job... digging tunnels deep under German positions on the Western Front. In his immaculate pencilled log, he charts the horrors of life in the trenches...

## 1916, France

**Jan 1** Arrived Rouen. Had several miles to march with full kit. Feeling pretty rough – effects of sea-sickness – had a bad dose.

**Jan 18** Had to dip water out of pond to wash, water nice and green. Ducked when I heard first shot. Germans 75 yards away.

**Jan 27** Our fellows pushed bundles of straw over parapet. Germans thought we were going to attack so they stood to their parapet. Our guns then opened rapid fire on them. Must have inflicted heavy losses.

**Jan 29** Lovely morning but cold and frosty. One would not think there was a war on. From one dug-out comes the smell of bacon frying, in another someone is playing a tin whistle and a little further on there are some pipers playing.

**Jan 30** Got paid yesterday: Ten francs for two weeks. Will have to go careful to make it last. Good dinner of beef steak and chips.

**Feb 14** My birthday today, 24, coming on bit. Last year I was a good many thousands of miles away. Wonder where I will be this time next year?

**Feb 23** Heavy snow and very hard frost. My leather coat was frozen as stiff as a board while I was wearing it. Everywhere you see fire buckets with a ring of soldiers in skin coats sitting round. Every spare bit of wood picked up for firewood.

**Feb 27** Can hear church bells ringing on one side and guns on the other. Graves everywhere behind trenches and in fields with farmers ploughing round them.

**Feb 28** This war game is rather exciting. You never know what's coming next.

John French survived the war and was awarded the Military Cross but died of TB in 1929, aged 37

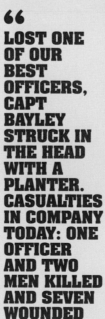

" LOST ONE OF OUR BEST OFFICERS, CAPT BAYLEY STRUCK IN THE HEAD WITH A PLANTER. CASUALTIES IN COMPANY TODAY: ONE OFFICER AND TWO MEN KILLED AND SEVEN WOUNDED "

**Mar 5** Could hear Germans working in their sap (underground gallery). They appear to be below us which is unusual. We are starting a rabbit hole right away to try to get below them. Instructions to be very careful, pad feet, speak in whispers and not to drop anything heavy.

**Mar 15** On one part of our mine there is a pretty smart German sniper and he has killed a number of our men.

**Mar 19** Hot sniper got another victim. Kept hitting sand bags in one place trying to work through.

**Mar 21** Sniper got two victims again today, two brothers they say.

**Mar 29** I think crack sniper must be killed for there has been no sniping for days.

**Apl 23** Soaking wet working in sap. Germans blew another mine this morning.

**Apl 24** In wet sap again working past the knees in water and water coming down your back like a shower bath. After about three hours air so

**Apl 16 One of our chaps killed by sniper. Forgot himself and put head above parapet. Got bullet clean through his head. Worked in darkness all night but had good sing song. Everyone seems in good spirits.**

bad that we had to come out – candles would not burn.

Apl 27 Germans sent over gas shells which burst 200 yards away. Sent out thick yellow smoke which rolled along like a fog bank, the wind driving it away. Went to doctor to see about a cut on the ankle. He said it was septic and sent me to hospital.

Apl 28 In hospital. Plenty of company, wounded coming in all the time.

May 22 One of the worst nights I've experienced. Regular nightmare.

May 23 Scores of men lying dead. You can see arms and legs sticking up everywhere. These grenades are murderous things.

June 1 Found a lot of water-cress growing in a stream – had some for tea. It went all right with the bread and cheese.

June 21 Had mouse in a cage with us in gallery so we would be warned if gas got very bad. We got enough gas to make us sick but mouse was still alive and kicking.

June 22 They got in our trenches but very few got back again. Enemy carried hand grenades and daggers beside rifle and bayonet. Party of our chaps got around and cut their retreat off. There was a German officer lying dead just over the back of our trench with a grenade still in his hand. Saw our chaps dressing wounds of a prisoner. Only a scratch but he was making a lot of fuss. Big chap too, over six feet.

Aug 10 Heard laughing and saw German leaning over parapet and shouting to our men who were also leaning over. One of our men shouted "come on over Fritz". Fritz shouted back in perfect English "no bloomin' fear". This went on for half an hour and then heads were down and war went on the same as usual. Instant death for first to put his head above the parapet.

Aug 13 Orders today that any German looking over

parapet is to be shot and any man found talking to them to be arrested.

Oct 29 Lost one of our best officers. Capt Bayley struck in the head with a planter. Casualties in company today: One officer and two men killed and seven wounded. Won't be many of us left soon at this rate.

Nov 5 Took stroll around foot of Abraham Heights. Scores of our chaps dead.

Nov 6 Another "push". Barrage was like a great fireworks display.

## 1917, Ypres

Oct 24 Had a nasty day of it today. We were marching single file when a shell burst in. The scene that followed was awful. Five were killed outright and seven wounded. Wounded were shouting and screaming for help. So many you hardly knew who to help first. Some had legs and arms blown off. Altogether a nightmare day.

Oct 28 Saw a very gallant deed today. Fritz dropped a shell on the road seriously injuring a rider. All the rest of the men bolted with the exception of one man who got the wounded man on his shoulders.

Nov 2 Heavy bombarding from Fritz this morning. Artillery men call it "morning hate". One man sitting eating his lunch on a pile of wood killed by a sniper. Bullet went straight through him.

Nov 17 Day off today. Good game of football and got licked 2-1. Weather better.

> **THEY GOT IN OUR TRENCHES BUT VERY FEW GOT OUT AGAIN. THERE WAS A GERMAN OFFICER LYING DEAD JUST OVER THE BACK OF OUR TRENCH WITH A GRENADE STILL IN HIS HAND**

Sappers seen here clearing the ground for a howitzer during the Third Battle of Ypres in 1917

# 'GERMANS SHOWED THE WHITE FLAG AND OUR MEN WENT TO TAKE THEM PRISONER... AND THEN THEY FIRED ON US'

From the "unbearable" reality of battle to the menace of fleas and an emotional farewell message to a young child, these letters provide a fascinating glimpse into the lives of soldiers serving on the front line.

Second Lieutenant Neville Leslie Woodroffe was sent to France in 1914, surviving the retreat from Mons and the Battle of Landrecies.

In his letter, he reveals an incident in which a group of Germans held up a white flag before opening fire, killing several of his comrades.

Sergeant Francis Herbert Gautier wrote a farewell letter to his young daughter Marie as he lay dying in hospital.

"I am writing because I want you to know how dearly I loved you," he wrote.

"I know that you are too young now to keep me in your memory."

Marie is asked her to "be a comfort" to her mother, who had also lost a son in the war.

George Nanzig, who was just 16 when he volunteered as a private, has a "good grumble" about life in the trenches in a letter to his mother.

A month after writing the message he was reported missing in action, presumed dead.

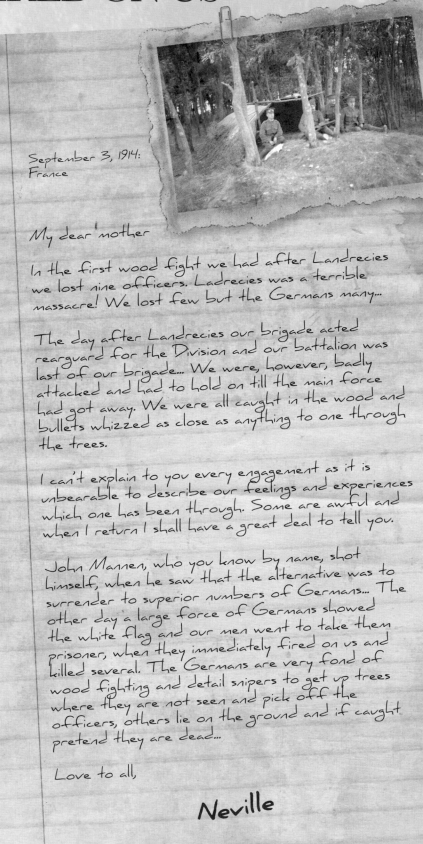

September 3, 1914: France

My dear mother

In the first wood fight we had after Landrecies we lost nine officers. Landrecies was a terrible massacre! We lost few but the Germans many....

The day after Landrecies our brigade acted rearguard for the Division and our battalion was last of our brigade... We were, however, badly attacked and had to hold on till the main force had got away. We were all caught in the wood and bullets whizzed as close as anything to one through the trees.

I can't explain to you every engagement as it is unbearable to describe our feelings and experiences which one has been through. Some are awful and when I return I shall have a great deal to tell you.

John Mannen, who you know by name, shot himself, when he saw that the alternative was to surrender to superior numbers of Germans.... The other day a large force of Germans showed the white flag and our men went to take them prisoner, when they immediately fired on us and killed several. The Germans are very fond of wood fighting and detail snipers to get up trees where they are not seen and pick off the officers, others lie on the ground and if caught pretend they are dead...

Love to all,

Neville

August 15, 1915: France

Dearly loved daughter Marie,

This, my letter to you, is written in grief. I had hoped to spend many happy years with you after the war was over and to see you grow into a good and happy woman. I am writing because I want you to know how dearly I loved you. I know that you are too young now to keep me in your memory. I know your dear Mother will grieve. Be a comfort to her, remember when you are old enough that she lost her dear son, your brother, and me, your father, within a short time. Your brother was a dear boy, honour his memory for he loved you (and) your brothers dearly and he died like a brave soldier in defence of his home and country.

May God guide and keep you safe and that at last we may all meet together in his eternal rest

I am your loving and affectionate father.

F.H. Gautier.

August 15, 1915: France

Dear Mum,

I hope this letter will find you in the same health as it leaves me at present. You know in the last letter I wrote we had just come out of the trenches and we were expecting to come right back for a well earned rest, well we have got it (in the trenches for another 14 days or more) – the bloke who says a soldier don't earn his bob a day should come where I am writing this letter and then give his opinion. Well Mum, I suppose we mustn't grumble, but a good grumble eases our mind. It is about 11 o'clock now and the skies look about black enough to give us enough rain to last us the whole time we are in. So I expect we shall soon be up to our necks in mud.

It is August now but it's blooming cold of a night time so goodness knows how it will be round Christmas time. Well Mum I wouldn't give a tuppence for sunny France as some people call it.

… I must close now as the fleas are irritating me so I must look at my shirt. I find millions of them every day, goodness knows where they all come from.

With love to you from your lousy,

George

**PERSONAL STORIES**

LETTERS FROM THE FRONT

# 'TOO OLD' ARTHUR RETURNS HOME A DOUBLE VC HERO

**M**ore than a decade after his selfless heroism during the Boer War had earned Arthur Martin-Leake a Victorian Cross, he was itching to get back to the frontline.

Fearing he would be considered too old to volunteer for the Western Front, he travelled to Paris and enlisted as a lieutenant with the 5th Field Ambulance, Royal Army Medical Corps.

Under heavy fire, the 40-year-old went on to rescue a large number of wounded soldiers lying close to the enemy's trenches, earning a second VC in the process.

The award meant he became the first person to be given Britain's highest honour for gallantry on two occasions.

Recommending him for a Bar to his VC, his commanding officer wrote: "By his devotion many lives have been saved that would otherwise undoubtedly have been lost.

"His behaviour on three occasions when the dressing station was heavily shelled was such as to inspire confidence both with the wounded and the staff.

"It is not possible to quote any one specific act performed because his gallant conduct was continual."

Born in April 1874, near Ware, Hertfordshire, Arthur was at Vlakfontein in the Transvaal on February 8, 1902, when he won his first VC.

He risked his life to treat a wounded man under intense fire with enemy riflemen

**Above** Arthur Martin-Leake, who was awarded the VC twice for his bravery during the Boer conflict and the First World War

**Right** Sidney Godley was held in a German prison camp for most of the war

just 100 yards away. Continuing to help the wounded men even after he'd been shot, the exhausted medic even refused water until all the soldiers had received some first.

After leaving the battlefields of South Africa, Arthur went on to become the chief medical officer with an Indian railway company, a role he returned to at the end of the First World War.

He later commanded a mobile Air Raid Precaution post during the Second World War and died, aged 79, at High Cross, Hertfordshire.

The heroic medic's little-known exploits were revealed after his military records were published online on the family tree website findmypast.co.uk.

He is commemorated with a plaque and a tree at the National Memorial Arboretum in Alrewas in Staffordshire.

# FIGHTING ON WITH BULLET IN HIS HEAD

**S**hot in the head while holding off the enemy, Sidney Godley's commanders recommended him for a posthumous Victoria Cross.

What they did not know was that the soldier had miraculously survived the suicidal last stand and was being held in a prison camp.

Sidney's extraordinary bravery allowed the pinned-down British Army to retreat from the advancing Germans in the first military action of the First World War.

The 25-year-old Royal Fusilier and Lieutenant Maurice Dease, 24, both volunteered to man a machine gun defending Nimy bridge in the Battle of Mons on August 23, 1914.

Maurice, also awarded a VC, was killed and Sidney, despite having shrapnel in his back and a bullet lodged in his skull, fought on.

He held the position for two hours before dismantling the gun and throwing the pieces into a canal before he was overrun by German soldiers.

Sidney, of East Grinstead, West Sussex, was operated on at a German field hospital and spent the rest of the conflict in captivity.

The first person to be awarded the VC in the war, he was finally presented with his medal at Buckingham Palace in 1919.

The recommendation by Lieutenant FWA Steele, Royal Fusiliers, states: "In the defence of a railway bridge near Nimy, 23rd August 1914, Private Godley of 'B' Company showed particular heroism in his management of the machine guns.

"His Commanding Officer having been severely wounded and each machine gunner in turn shot, Private Godley was called to the firing line on the bridge and under heavy fire he had to remove three dead bodies and proceed to an advanced machine gun position under a sustained enemy fire.

"He carried on defending the position for two hours after he had received a severe head wound."

Sidney, whose medal was sold for £276,000 at auction in 2012, married Ellen in 1919 and was a school caretaker for 30 years.

He retired and they moved to Debden, Essex. He died in 1957. There is a plaque with his name on the bridge in Belgium.

## GOODBYE LETTER TO 'DARLING' WIFE

Sir Winston Churchill wrote a poignant letter to his wife to open if he died in the First World War trenches. Churchill, who wrote it to Clementine on July 17, 1915, as he headed to the Western Front, declares his love for her – and begs her not to mourn him too deeply.

It adds: "Do not grieve for me too much. Death is only an incident, & not the most important. Since I met you my darling one I have been happy, & you have taught me how noble a woman's heart can be. If there is anywhere else I shall be on the look out for you.

"Meanwhile look forward, feel free, rejoice in Life, cherish the children, guard my memory. God bless you. Good bye." Churchill had served as Home Secretary and First Admiralty Lord but was forced to resign from the Government after he was blamed for the disastrous Gallipoli campaign – and chose active service as a Lieutenant Colonel commanding the 6th Battalion Royal Scots Fusiliers.

## SECRET EXPLOITS

A quiet bank manager's family were stunned to learn he was a First World War hero who fought behind enemy lines for three days.

Corporal Reginald "Rex" Billingham died in 1965 never having told his wife Susan or daughter Beryl about his heroism. His exploits only came to light when a historian discovered a journal he wrote in 1960. Reginald was stranded in a shell hole after his battalion, the 2nd Honourable Artillery Company, tried to recapture Bullecourt, a northern French village, in May 1917. Surrounded by German troops, he survived mortar fire for four nights before dodging a hail of bullets to return to British troops. Awarded the Military Medal, he went on to become a Barclays bank manager in St Alban's, Herts.

# 'WELCOME TO THE WESTERN FRONT'

**Henry Bodkin gets a taste of life in the trenches as he goes on a mission to find out what British Tommies had to go through while on the front line**

"**K**eep your head down!" screams the burly sergeant major as I edge forward from the communications trench towards the front line.

"You are surrounded on three sides by 'Jerry'. If you stick your head above the parapet, you will be dead."

I crouch and try to advance down the trench but my feet will not move. They have disappeared, clamped into the light brown, gluey mud. I look around for something to hold so I can yank myself free.

"Don't touch that!" explodes the same voice. "Do not touch anything! Anything you touch will cut you. If you get cut you will be infected."

He is right. What is not splintering wood is rusting corrugated iron. I eye up a thick cord running along the side of the trench but am told this is the 'sacrosanct' telephone line, whose safety is more important than my own or any other soldiers'.

Somehow I squelch, slide and contort myself forward until I am squatting on what is allegedly the floor of the most forward front line trench. "Welcome to the Western Front," says Sergeant Major Craig Appleton.

The trench wall is an odd constellation of wooden boards, metal panels and sandbags, seemingly held together by, and smeared over, with this endless, sticky mud. Behind me a suffocating passage leads into a gloomy, damp dug-out, where I can just make out a forlorn candle flickering in the corner below

the thin smoke from a charcoal stove. Back in the trench the wall nearest the 'enemy' is lined with a 2ft-high layer of sandbags, which forms a firing step. On it stands Private Ryan Gearing, hunched over a periscope which pokes above the trench's lip. Everything is wet.

Such would have been the introduction for a new recruit to the British front line at Ypres in 1917. But I am not in war-ravaged Belgium, neither am I an apprehensive young Tommy.

It is 2014 and I am on a scruffy piece of land at Windacres Farm near the village of Charlwood, just outside Gatwick Airport.

Due to the painstaking efforts of military historian Andrew Robertshaw, however, this replica portion of a British Great War trench, gives probably a more accurate and vivid impression of what faced our war-time Army than any museum.

Every detail, dimension, proportion and material is an authentic replica of the British line at Ypres. Built in 2012, the project is a labour of love for Andrew, who is the curator of the Royal Logistics Corps Museum at Deepcut and was an adviser on Steven Spielberg's blockbuster film War Horse.

"I once met a veteran who said his war was 90% bored stiff, 9% frozen stiff and 1% scared stiff," he says. "What we are looking to highlight here is that 99%, not the 1%. I am not just fascinated by the battles – the going over the top surrounded by bursting shells, shrapnel and torrents of machine-gun bullets. I'm interested in the day-to-day experience of the ordinary British soldier in the trenches."

Together with his band of like-minded experts, such as former Met detective, and historical Army kit consultant Craig Appleton, military publisher Ryan Gearing and playwright and actor Alex Gwyther, Andrew aims to turn his trench complex into

Craig Appleton sitting inside a cold and damp bunker that doubled as a command post

a resource for students and teachers to learn about the reality of the Great War in Britain.

The most striking feature of the trenches is just how much it shows that the Tommies were fighting two parallel campaigns: one against the Germans and the other against their own environment. Walls were constantly sagging, subsiding and outright collapsing.

Soldiers also fought a nonstop battle against flooding in their trenches during the rainy months. The endless, back-breaking work needed to keep a trench in good enough shape to live and fight in was bad enough.

But it all had to be done from a crouching position, or in the pitch black of night, with the threat of the enemy ever-present.

Even basic tasks such as hammering in nails were fraught with danger, as a repetitive noise from a single position could attract the murderous attention of an enemy artillery spotter. This reality would have been some shock to the keen-spirited, broad-chested recruits inspired by Lord Kitchener's posters.

Instead of the dashing and glorious actions of the imperial past, they found themselves engaged in a vicious, subterranean scramble for small advantages. A good demonstration of this was the practice of placing men in forward listening posts: small holes dug into No Man's Land and accessible only by a shallow channel barely wide enough to crawl through.

The sentries posted there provided a crucial early warning mechanism for their mates back in the trench. But in the event of an assault they would almost certainly be wiped out.

Back at Charlwood, Alex demonstrates this, lying flat as a pancake in the listening position, the dome of his helmet just visible against the tangle of 'friendly' barbed wire that stands between him and the British trench. In the event of an attack, a listener who stood up to dash back into his trench was just as likely to get mown down by his own side as by the Germans.

The only alternative would be to slither backwards down the access slit and under the barbed wire. Amid the furious pace of an enemy attack, Alex would not have stood a chance. Grim stuff – but at least his job is one intended to fight the enemy.

Just a few yards behind him, the passage between the communication and front line trenches has collapsed. Sergeant Major Appleton has joined Private Gearing with a stubby entrenching tool to try to furrow a plausible passage out of the mess.

Together, almost in slow motion, they slither and slide around the muddy trifle, more like tipsy snails in uniform than soldiers of King George. Between them and Alex, lying flat in No Man's Land listening out for Jerry, you begin to get an idea of the strange, lethal and almost comic lifestyle of the Great War Army.

At first glance a tour of the Charlwood trench might seem like a weekend option only for the eccentric or mildly disturbed. But this is no gaudy re-enactment society or bunch of crackpots playing in the garden. The men who make the Charlwood trench special do so because their fearsome knowledge of their subject and attention to detail is matched only by their reverence for the Army whose actions, lifestyle and daily heroism they seek to understand and explain.

**Above left**
Alex Gwyther quietly lies in a forward listening post, a position that often proved fatal for the soldiers in the war

**Above right**
Ryan Gearing and Craig Appleton going 'over the top'

**" THE SENTRIES PROVIDED A CRUCIAL EARLY WARNING MECHANISM FOR THEIR MATES BACK IN THE TRENCH. BUT IN THE EVENT OF AN ASSAULT THEY WOULD ALMOST CERTAINLY BE WIPED OUT "**

# 'NOT A DAY PASSES WITHOUT DEATH TAKING HIS TOLL'

**PERSONAL STORIES**

EDITH APPLETON

**Nurse Edith Appleton spent four years treating wounded soldiers in France and Belgium and kept fascinating diaries of her experiences. In these extracts, which cover the Battle of the Somme, she writes a courageous account of life on the front line of trench warfare**

**July 2, 1916** The last eight days the guns have been firing the whole time. Fine big ones they must be for us to hear them so distinctly, and how the china must be rattling at the clearing stations! The Germans have been giving themselves up and coming across in dazed groups – which is fine. How absolutely glorious if we knock them right out and level them flat, so our infantry and cavalry can have a walkover such as would make good reading in history.

**July 3** Our much-longed for advance has begun after many days of heavy bombardment, and we launched an attack at 7.30 on Saturday morning. They went over in waves, the second one so many minutes after the first, and so on. Where one man from the first wave was wiped out, so was the second, which gave the Germans time to adjust their machine guns to receive the rest. After the second wave they began to make headway and had them fairly on the run. We took the front line trenches for a distance of 25 miles and actually took the four front lines but had to retire to the first because they had the range of the other three and started shelling them.

**July 4** Wounded! Hundreds upon hundreds on stretchers, being carried, walking – all covered from head to foot in well-caked mud. We had horribly bad wounds in numbers – some crawling with maggots, some stinking and tense with gangrene. One poor lad had both eyes shot through and there they were, all smashed and mixed up with the eyelashes. He was quite calm, and very tired. He said, 'Shall I need an operation? I can't see anything.' Poor boy, he never will.

**July 6** I give up trying to describe it – it beats me. In ordinary times we get a telegraph from Abbeville saying a train with so many on board

> **WE HAD HORRIBLY BAD WOUNDS IN NUMBERS – SOME CRAWLING WITH MAGGOTS. ONE POOR LAD HAD HAD BOTH EYES SHOT THROUGH. SAID, 'SHALL I NEED AN OPERATION? I CAN'T SEE ANYTHING.' POOR BOY, HE NEVER WILL**

has left and is coming to us. Then they stopped giving numbers – just said 'full train'. Not even a telegram comes – but the full trains do.

**July 8** It is to be hoped our attacking is doing useful work for the war as we are paying a tall price! Every day now we have train-fulls coming down – the place is thick and threefold with them. The surgeons are amputating limbs and boring through skulls at the rate of 30 a day – and not a day passes without Death taking his toll.

**July 10** Standing at the door of any ward you hear the continuous plea from all sides for water, a drink – anything to drink – and all of us are giving drink as much as we possibly can, as well as doing the other jobs. Many men have told me that after our men have attacked, the Germans sweep the ground low with a machine gun to kill our wounded. I should think that this is an act best left to God to reward.

**July 13** Yesterday was a very busy day – a convoy in first thing and one sent out in the afternoon to be ready for the next one. I had only 63 of yesterday's convoy – two too ill to go on for a time, and I fear one boy may not get better. He has pneumonia caused by a lump of lead in his left lung. He is so blue and bad, poor dear.

Nurse Edith Appleton, who was born in Kent, died in 1958 at the age of 80

**July 31** Not a glimmer of hope for my poor boy Lennox. He has a generally poisoned condition and is daily weaker and worse. He has been good but now is so tired I think he will be glad of a rest.

**August 4** Had a letter from the mother of my ill boy. She asks that he may write just two words to her and she will feel more content. So I went back to the ward last night, in case he is not there this morning, and helped him to do it. It is a poor little five-word scrawl, but I hope it will please her poor soul.

......................................................

**August 12** It's 31 days since Lennox came in, and he is still not able to get away. He won't be long though, as the bad chest attacks are more frequent now and poor dear, he will be so grateful to be gone.

......................................................

**August 23** Lennox died soon after 8 o'clock last night. Never have I seen such a slow, painful death. It was as if the boy was chained to Earth for punishment. Towards the end it was agony for him to draw his little gasping breaths. I am very glad for the boy to be away.

......................................................

**September 11** We had a convoy of 399 in yesterday, but only 70 wounded. By far the majority of the sick were suffering badly from shell shock. It is sad to see them – they dither like palsied old men and talk all the time about their mates who were blown to bits, or their mates who were wounded and never brought in. The whole scene is burnt into their brains and they can't get rid of the sight of it. One rumpled, raisin-faced old fellow said his job was to take bombs up to the bombers, and sometimes going through the trenches he had to push past men with their arms blown off or horribly wounded, and they would yell at him, 'Don't touch me,' but he had to get past because the fellows must have their bombs. Then he would stand on something wobbly and nearly fall down – and see it was a dying or dead man, half covered in mud. Once he returned to find his own officer blown to bits – a leg in once place, his body in another. Another man told me quite calmly, "Our Div was terribly cut up, because we had to be a sacrifice to let the others advance... and they did advance all right."

......................................................

**September 12** The tales the men from the Somme tell are terrible – how some poor fellows go mad, and some die from fright or shock – and all swear terribly. One very quiet man told me swearing was not his habit, or any joy to him, but he swore as much as any man when shells were coming over. "It helps one to bear it quite wonderfully," he said.

......................................................

**September 19** We were called at 4am yesterday to admit a heavy convoy of wounded from the latest action. There were only 115 walkers, all the rest were badly wounded. Among mine there is one boy with his leg in such an awful state that I think it will have to come off, and on his chest there is a deep, wide wound about eight inches long, and both his arms are wounded. The two beside him have wounds right through their chest, and another man in the same room has his intestines sticking out through his ribs. However, they all seem very cheerful about things.  So far the Germans seem to be living right well and the

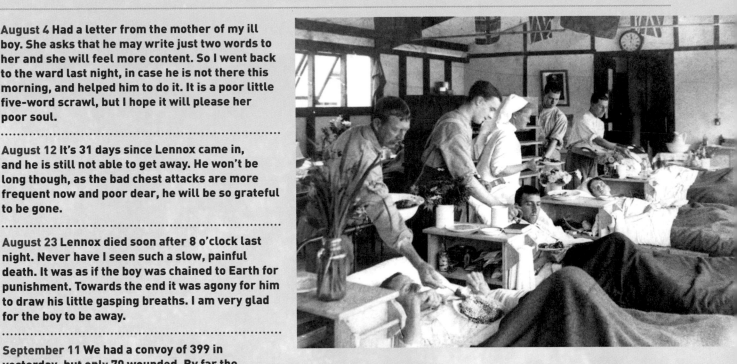

Tommies have found wine, cigars, soda water and other comforts in their front line trenches. Their dugouts are like wonderful underground hotels with bathrooms, hot and cold water, electric light and more!

......................................................

**October 1** We had a convoy of 347 in yesterday – badly wounded with only a dozen walking cases among them, so although numbers were not high, there was a great deal of work and we are all going on after first breakfast. I only took 43 patients – German prisoners. They always fall to my share. Six were slight cases, but the rest were shot to rags and putrid! Really the smell of gangrene, added to the always unpleasant German smell, was a trial to one's stomach.

......................................................

**October 3** My German prisoners are as happy as sandboys – they sing and laugh and talk, and some seem to be really nice men. They are most grateful for all that is done for them and their stinking wounds are cleaning up wonderfully.

......................................................

**October 10** Had a man brought in who was so badly wounded across the shoulders that both arms were entirely paralysed. His story is pathetic. He was a servant to a major and at the attack they were both wounded. They were together getting over the parapet, and quite soon the major was hit in the lungs. Mac carried him to the nearest shelter – just a shell hole – but soon found that unsafe, so he carried him further back. He settled him in a little nook then sat close to shelter him. After a bit Mac got hit and found he was unable to do anything for the major using his arms, but he stayed on, although he might well have walked to the dressing station and had his own wounds attended to. He stayed, doing what he could for the major by nosing round him like a dog and using his teeth, and eventually after 12 hours the stretcher-bearers came. They took the major first – and he was caught by another shell and killed. When the stretcher-bearers went back they found Mac unconscious, having been hit again.

Some of the soldiers who were wounded during the first day of the Somme offensive, seen here in hospital receiving lunch on their ward

"

**THE TALES THE MEN FROM THE SOMME TELL ARE TERRIBLE – HOW SOME POOR FELLOWS GO MAD, AND SOME DIE FROM FRIGHT OR SHOCK – AND ALL SWEAR TERRIBLY** "

# WAR HERO WHO HAD WORLD AT HIS FEET

**Walter Tull gave up a promising football career to fight for his country and went on to become the British Army's first black officer. He died a hero but the reason why he never received a bravery medal remains a mystery. Claudia Tanner tells his inspirational story...**

Growing up in an orphanage after losing both parents before his ninth birthday, Walter Tull was no stranger to overcoming adversity.

Born in April 1888 in Kent, his school reports suggested he was "a stoic, laid-back character but single-minded". It was a set of personality traits that would help make the grandson of Barbadian slaves a success on the football pitch and in the military.

As a teenager he was an inside-forward for Clapton FC. After helping the team to win a hatful of trophies, he was snapped up by Tottenham Hotspur, making him the first black outfield player in England's top division.

However, Tull must have stood out in lily-white Britain. A report on a Bristol City v Spurs match in 1909 is believed to have made the first ever mention of racial abuse at a professional football game.

The Football Star newspaper reported: "A section of the spectators made a cowardly attack on him in language lower than Billingsgate [London's fish market].

"Let me tell those Bristol hooligans that Tull is so clean in mind and method as to be a model for all white men who play football."

It is believed that racial hostility from rival fans led to Walter making just 10 appearances for Spurs' first team, and he was later sold to Northampton Town.

A move to Glasgow Rangers was on the cards before war broke out, with Walter deciding to volunteer for the 17th

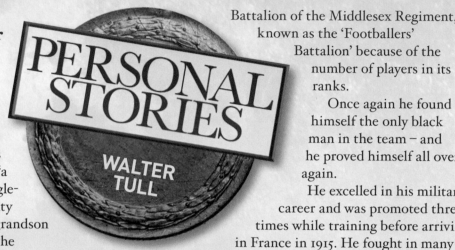

PERSONAL STORIES

WALTER TULL

Walter Tull was on the verge of joining Glasgow Rangers when war broke out in 1914

Battalion of the Middlesex Regiment, known as the 'Footballers' Battalion' because of the number of players in its ranks.

Once again he found himself the only black man in the team – and he proved himself all over again.

He excelled in his military career and was promoted three times while training before arriving in France in 1915. He fought in many fierce operations, including the Battle of the Somme in 1916, and from there he was sent to the Italian Front. After one daring night raid, in which Walter led 26 men across a swirling river and brought them all back unharmed, he was mentioned in despatches for "gallantry and coolness under fire".

Walter was recommended for promotion and he won his officer's commission in May 1917 – despite military regulations preventing any "person of colour" being given the position – becoming the British Army's first black officer.

Philip Vasili, author of Walter Tull, 1888-1918, Officer, Footballer: All the Guns in France Couldn't Wake Me, says: "It's a testament to his character – his natural leadership skills – that he became an officer, despite it being against the rules.

"Walter was a calm, very grounded, quietly reserved individual. He was a man of action not a man of words. It's something of a contradiction – he faced difficulties in terms of racism, but it also shows the

**Above** Walter Tull, bottom right, pictured with his Spurs teammates in 1910

**Far left** British troops negotiate a trench In support of an attack during the Battle of the Somme, which Walter took part in

**Left** The memorial in Northampton

progressive elements coming through in the British."

By the spring of 1918, Walter was back on the Somme and, on March 25, Walter vanished into a hail of gunfire and exploding shells in No Man's Land. His body was never found. He was 29. Walter's name had been put forward for the Military Cross in recognition of his bravery in Italy, according to letters sent to his family after he was killed. But the soldier never received the award, fuelling speculation he had been overlooked because military chiefs would have been embarrassed to see the medal on a black man's uniform. The Ministry of Defence said no record of the Military Cross recommendation was found in Walter's service files.

"Of course I can't prove it but I think if they had given him his medal it would have almost validated the legal status of a black officer and they would have had to change the rules, and they didn't want to do that," says Mr Vasili.

He wants Walter to be posthumously awarded the medal, a campaign supported by the soldier's relatives, including his great nephew, Edward Finlayson.

"In our family, we were always very proud of Walter and we knew my grandfather's brother was the first black professional outfield player," says the 62-year-old. "But it was only since he's gained notoriety, if that's the right word, that we learned that he was the very first black officer in the Army."

There is a memorial to Walter in Northampton Town's garden of remembrance, and there are plans to make a film about his life.

> " IT'S A TESTAMENT TO HIS CHARACTER – HIS NATURAL LEADERSHIP SKILLS – THAT HE BECAME AN OFFICER, DESPITE IT BEING AGAINST THE RULES "

# 'I'LL BE BACK'... PRISONER KEEPS PROMISE HE GAVE TO GERMANY'S KAISER

**Right** British prisoners of war under guard at a camp in Doeberitz, near Berlin

**Below** Captain Robert Campbell. Reproduced by permission of Surrey History Centre

**A** British soldier at a First World War prison camp was allowed to visit his dying mother on one condition – that he returned to his German captors.

Captain Robert Campbell was granted leave after he wrote to Kaiser Wilhelm II begging to see her one last time.

Astonishingly, the officer kept his promise to the German leader and came back after travelling home to Kent.

Historian Richard van Emden discovered the curious tale when researching for his book, Meeting The Enemy: The Human Face of the Great War.

He says: "People may say it's amazing that the Kaiser let this man go and that he returned to Germany.

"I find it amazing that the British Army let him go back. Kaiser Wilhelm II had a love-hate relationship with Britain – he was Queen Victoria's grandson and there's a lot he adored about the country.

"He likely saw this as a one-off gesture which Britain would reciprocate."

As for the officer, Mr van Emden says that he would have felt a duty to return.

"He would have given his word that he would return to Germany and, as an officer, this would have been something he honoured," he says.

"It's likely he would have thought this was the start of soldiers being given leave on both sides and that by not going back he could scupper the chances for other people."

Robert, of the 1st Battalion East Surrey Regiment, was

captured in northern France on August 24, 1914, just weeks after Britain joined the war.

He was treated in a military hospital in Cologne, Germany, before being transported to a prisoner of war camp in Magdeburg.

While in the camp he received news that his mother, Louise, was dying of cancer and was granted leave.

He reached his mother's bedside in Gravesend in Kent on December 7, 1916, and spent a week with her before returning to Germany. She eventually died two months later.

Mr van Emden unearthed the unusual story as he researched correspondence between the British Foreign Office and its German counterparts.

He also discovered the British turned down a similar request for a German soldier Peter Gastreich to be allowed to leave the Isle of Wight to see his dying mother.

The author reveals that Robert and a group of other prisoners spent nine months digging their way out of the camp before being captured on the Dutch border.

"I've not come across any research to suggested Capt Campbell particularly complained about his treatment at the camp," he says. "Conditions for PoWs varied greatly depending on the time it was in the war and the country.

"As long as you didn't antagonise the guards, officers generally fared better than ordinary soldiers because their living conditions were on the whole of a higher standard and they were not required to work.

"Capt Campbell escaped because PoWs had a duty to try to escape. Once he fulfilled his promise to return, he was simply doing his duty again."

At the end of the war, Robert was released and returned to Britain.

He was again thrust into action at the outbreak of the Second World War in 1939, serving as the chief observer of the Royal Observer Corps on the Isle of Wight. He died in July 1966, aged 81.

## " HE WOULD HAVE GIVEN HIS WORD THAT HE WOULD RETURN TO GERMANY AND, AS AN OFFICER, THIS WOULD HAVE BEEN SOMETHING HE HONOURED "

# SILK HANDKERCHIEF CLUE TO SECRET WAR EXPLOITS OF 'SNOWY'

Life in the trenches was tough – but machine gunner Harry Foulger still found time to send romantic tokens home to his sweetheart.

Margaret – the woman for whom he picked out a white silk handkerchief – was later to become his wife of 50 years.

Harry joined the Army in 1913 and fought all over France.

His granddaughter Julie, of Welwyn, Hertfordshire, proudly displays on her wall the four service medals he received, as well as a commendation from King George V.

But alongside is the hankie, embroidered with the dates 1914-1915 and the words, "Je tonne pour le droit" (I'm gunning for justice).

It wasn't until Margaret died in 1992, aged 94, that the family had any idea Harry had fought for his country.

"Once, as a young child, my mother remembered finding a cardboard tube in a cupboard," remembers Julie, now 69.

"My nan smacked her on the wrist and told her never to talk about it again.

"But when we were going through her stuff we found the tube and in it was his citation from the Army.

"Then we found the pictures of him in uniform and finally the handkerchief.

"It was an emotional experience to discover all that about him so long after the event."

Pictures from 1915 show Harry – known as Snowy thanks to his hair turning white at an early age – surrounded by fellow soldiers of the 1st Cambridgeshire Regiment.

He survived the war and the bloody Battle of the Somme unscathed, and returned home to become a cabinet maker.

He married Margaret in 1919 and in 1923 their only child, Barbara, was born. Harry died in 1973 at the age of 77 without ever revealing he was a war hero.

# FLYING ACE A SENSITIVE SOUL WITH DEADLY AIM

**Edward 'Mick' Mannock overcame a nervous start to become Britain's highest-scoring WW1 fighter pilot, writes Claudia Tanner**

**O**riginally seen as a coward by his fellow pilots, Edward 'Mick' Mannock ended up shooting down more German planes than any other British airman during the First World War.

The flying ace had more than 60 air combat victories to his name – and was known for his ruthless treatment of anyone who crossed his path.

"Hating the enemy was not uncommon of course but Mannock seemed to take delight in killing them," says his biographer, Andy Saunders. "He would say 'Flamerinoes boys! Sizzle sizzle wonk' as he described how he shot them down in flames.

"He certainly would have lost friends to the Germans and resentment would have built up. It could also possibly be because he was so badly treated by the Turks – Germany's WWI ally – when he was working as a telephone engineer in Turkey and interned by them earlier in the war."

Maj Mannock once forced a German two-seater to crash, then repeatedly machine-gunned the helpless crew. Yet the ace was a walking contradiction – behind this seemingly brutal exterior was a sensitive soul.

His personal diary, held at the RAF Museum in London, shows Maj Mannock was struggling to control his nerves from the moment he went into action.

"Feeling nervy and ill during

*Above right, a dog fight during the First World War. Edward 'Mick' Mannock, below, had more than 60 air combat victories to his name*

the last week. Afraid I'm breaking up," it read.

Maj Mannock was born to corporal Edward Mannock and an Irish mother, Julia, possibly on May 24, 1887, in Brighton, although there is no record of this and it is thought by some that he may have been born in Ireland. In 1915, he joined the Royal Army Medical Corps and became an officer in the Royal Engineers before transferring to the Royal Flying Corps.

Flying aircraft during the First World War was a shockingly dangerous profession. Of the 14,000 airmen killed in the conflict, more than half lost their lives in training, and their life expectancy was just a few weeks.

"It was a very, very risky profession. There were no parachutes in the First World War so when they were shot down, that was often the end, says Mr Saunders. "Mannock's fellow pilots didn't believe he had what it took at first and believed he was 'windy' – or in other words a coward. But he found his feet and gained more confidence when he became more prolific in flying and shooting down the enemy."

Maj Mannock worked tirelessly to overcome his fears and hone his craft and shot down a German observation balloon on May 7, 1917. The kills soon came thick and fast – along with 'ace status' – and with them came the awards for gallantry.

On September 17 that year he won the Military Cross for driving off several German aircraft while also downing three German balloons. Astonishing, in May 1918, Maj Mannock shot down 20

German planes and won the Distinguished Service Order three times in little over a month.

Maj Mannock's comrade and fellow ace Ira Jones claimed his friend had 73 victories but he is officially credited with 61. It has been said that he seldom claimed the credit for kills when assisting newer pilots.

Despite his undeniable skill and the bravado, it seems Maj Mannock became deeply affected by the carnage. After he shot down a German plane and found one of the airmen dead inside, he wrote in his diary that he "felt exactly like a murderer". He also records visiting the site where one of his victims had crashed near the front line and describes the sight of "dead men's legs sticking through the sides with puttees and boots still on – bits of bones and skulls with the hair peeling off" as "rather nauseating".

He continues: "This sort of thing, together with the strong graveyard stench and the dead and mangled body of the pilot combined to upset me for a few days."

He became especially distressed when he saw one of his victims catch fire while crashing to the ground. From then on, he always kept a revolver in his cockpit. He told his friend, Lieutenant MacLanachan: "The reason I bought it was to finish myself as soon as I see the first signs of flames. They'll never burn me."

> **WE DO KNOW THAT HE CARRIED A REVOLVER TO END IT ALL IF HE SHOULD BE BROUGHT DOWN IN FLAMES**

By the summer of 1918, the savagery of the air war had become too much to bear. The flying ace was found by a friend trembling and sobbing while on leave. Nevertheless, he returned to France to fulfil his duty to his country.

Tragically, just days after warning a fellow ace about the deadly hazards of flying low into ground fire, Maj Mannock did just that on July 26, 1918. His plane was set on fire and he was killed in action aged 31. He was posthumously awarded the Victoria Cross the following year.

"We do know for a fact that his body was recovered and buried by the Germans," says Mr Saunders, the co-author of Mannock: The Life and Death of Major Edward Mannock VC, DSO, MC, RAF. "There is good evidence that a grave in Laventie, France, which is registered as 'Unknown Airman' by the Commonwealth War Graves Commission, is in fact Mannock's. It matches the location of where the Germans said they buried him.

"Mannock certainly went down with his aeroplane on fire, and we do know that he carried a revolver to end it all if he should be brought down in flames. It is entirely possible that he did just that but we will never know.

"A great deal about this man's life and death is shrouded in some mystery, and perhaps that is all part of the great fascination with this true hero of World War One."

# The golden rules for flying in combat

Despite major advances in planes leading up to 1939, Maj Mannock's 15 air combat rules were used in the Second World War such was their importance to fighter pilots.

• Pilots must dive to attack with zest, and must hold their fire until they get within 100 yards of their target.

• Achieve surprise by approaching from the east (from the German side of the front).

• Utilize the sun's glare and clouds to achieve surprise.

• Pilots must keep physically fit by exercise and the moderate use of stimulants.

• Pilots must sight their guns and practice as much as possible as targets are normally fleeting.

• Pilots must practice spotting machines in the air and recognizing them at long range, and every aeroplane is to be treated as an enemy until it is certain it is not.

• Pilots must learn where the enemy's blind spots are.

• Scouts must be attacked from above and two-seaters from beneath their tails.

• Pilots must practice quick turns, as this manoeuvre is more used than any other in a fight.

• Pilots must practice judging distances in the air as these are very deceptive.

• Decoys must be guarded

against — a single enemy is often a decoy — therefore the air above should be searched before attacking.

• If the day is sunny, machines should be turned with as little bank as possible, otherwise the sun glistening on the wings will give away their presence at a long range.

• Pilots must keep turning in a dog fight and never fly straight except when firing.

• Pilots must never dive away from an enemy, as he gives his opponent a non-deflection shot – bullets are faster than aeroplanes.

• Pilots must keep their eye on their watches during patrols, and on the direction and strength of the wind.

# 'WE ONLY MISSED THE BOMB BY 10 MINUTES...'

**The outbreak of war in 1914 was followed by four years of turmoil. From her North London home, which she shared with husband George, Lillie Scales recorded it all in the pages of her diary, providing a fascinating insight into life on the home front**

PERSONAL STORIES

LILLE SCALES

## 1914

**August 3:** We heard that Germany had declared war on France and had invaded France, Luxembourg and Belgium, and we felt it must mean war for us and yet we felt that it would have been more natural to be fighting on Germany's side than against her. We little knew what her soul was like.

**August 4:** I went down to the grocer's and ordered in about £30 of provisions. On the stroke of 12pm, having waited till the last moment for Germany's reply to her note, Great Britain declared war on Germany. There was no alternative in honour.

**August 7:** I went up to the polytechnic for first aid classes. In my class there were 200 ladies. Everything was in the greatest confusion. Over 1,000 ladies had come, and they had not expected more than 50. We had five lectures on consecutive days on first aid – and then there was an exam. I did not take it, as it was absurd to rush it like that, and if I had managed to pass, I should not have remembered anything. The next week, five lectures on home nursing and an exam. Absurd, and the classes were too large to practise bandaging etc.

**August 8:** The recruiting offices were besieged and one of the saddest and yet most thrilling sights to me was to see parties of those young fellows who had just volunteered being marched from the recruiting office – perhaps 30, 50 or 100 of them – in all sorts of dress – top hats,

*Lillie Scales, below, turned up for a first-aid class with a thousand other women after the outbreak of war*

caps, soft hats, morning coats, jackets, shabby men and 'nuts', labourers, clerks, partners in great city businesses – hooligans, all mixed up, marching side by side, all having made the great decision, ready to lay down their lives for their country, and you could see this in many of their faces.

**October:** The Belgian refugees began to come over in such numbers that private hospitality was asked for them, and the response was wonderful. We all felt that it was owing to Belgium that our own land had been saved from the cruel Huns and that the sorrows and sufferings of Belgium would have been ours too if it had not been for the bravery of them and their King.

## 1915

Our first experience of a (Zeppelin) raid was on Tuesday, August 17. We had been spending the evening at Wanstead and, as they had no timetable, we had 20 minutes to wait at Leytonstone Station. The station is high and we noticed how black the night was. There had been a raid a few weeks before, and all gas lamps in London were blacked and shop windows and house windows darkened with shaded lights and heavy curtains. The penalty is very heavy for a naked light.

Many gas lamps in the street are turned out altogether and the roads are as black as pitch. You cannot see the edges of the pavement, and you knock into people. Many people

The damage following a German air raid in King's Lynn in 1916

carry little electric flashlights but in some neighbourhoods these are not allowed. The streets are really dangerous and it is said that there have been more accidents through the darkened streets than through Zeppelins. We have known of several personally.

Well, it was a very dark night and we took the 9.52 train. Twelve minutes later, just as we were coming up Hornsey Rise, we heard several muffled bangs, and saw curious flashes of light. People ran out of their houses. I thought of guns, but not of bombs, but the next morning we heard that we had just missed a dreadful raid at Leyton.

We went the following Saturday to see the damage done. All the glass of Leyton station was broken, and streets of houses had all the glass of the windows smashed, but it was very extraordinary in how many instances the bombs themselves had fallen in the road, or in yards. Many fell on Wanstead flats. Not many lives were lost. We saw a hole made by a bomb large enough for a cart to go in it. We only missed it by 10 minutes.

## 1916

Lloyd George was made Minister of Munitions, a new office, and the way in which he took matters in hand was wonderful, and a matter of history.

Now there are many hundred, there may even be thousands, of munition factories.

Lloyd George used to be our pet abomination but he is the man now whom everyone turns to, and feels confident in, whether as Chancellor of the Exchequer, Minister of Munitions, settler of trade disputes and now Prime Minister.

He who used to inveigh against the idle useless rich and aristocracy, now sees the aristocracy freely shedding its blood and doing its all for the country, while he had to go down to South Wales to implore 200,000 miners – who said they would as soon have the Kaiser as King George over them – to remember their brothers laying down their lives for them and that they, through refusing to work, were responsible for the lives of thousands. I think his point of view must have changed.

At the end of 1916 the Asquith ministry fell and nearly everyone was glad for everyone felt that more energy was needed and Lloyd George was welcomed as Prime Minister.

Five years ago we should have thought it impossible that our hopes would be centred in him, and now reforms of all kinds are being pressed forward.

At present the war has touched people in our class of life wonderfully little, except when those near and dear have gone to the front, but now it is coming nearer to us.

> **" AT THE END OF 1916 THE ASQUITH MINISTRY FELL AND NEARLY EVERYONE WAS GLAD FOR EVERYONE FELT THAT MORE ENERGY WAS NEEDED AND LLOYD GEORGE WAS WELCOMED AS PRIME MINISTER "**

## 1917

There is no doubt that the war has a very depressing effect. I am sure it has caused my dear father's illness. There is no doubt it has affected both him and Mother very much. It is very sad for old people, and they cannot shake off the gloom even as younger people can, though one always has a sense of trouble and evil hanging over oneself. Theatres are very full, but mostly with soldiers and their friends.

There is a super tax of 2d in the shilling on all tickets for entertainments. I think I have only been twice since the war began to a theatre. We have given no Christmas or other presents since the war began. The streets are so dark that unless the moon is shining you cannot see a thing.

Very few lights are lit, and those almost all blacked or greened, and I would not go out at night without my little electric torch. But one never hears a word from anyone about giving in. I don't think it ever occurs to anyone.

**April 13:** We have all been greatly thrilled by America's entry into the war. President

> **THE FOOD SITUATION IS MUCH THE SAME, AND IS NOT LIKELY TO VARY MUCH AT PRESENT, NOR ARE PRICES EXPECTED TO COME DOWN MUCH YET, BUT – THE WAR IS OVER!**

A shortage of food led to the introduction of compulsory rationing in January 1918. Below, disappointed shoppers outside a butcher's shop

Wilson made a great speech. Many people say that, though the morale effect will be great, there will not be an appreciable difference made to the war by the Americans joining, but there must be.

**July 22:** Since I last wrote in this book, my dear father has passed away. At 11 o'clock at night on May 26th, he entered into fuller life. I, and we all, are sure that the depression and anxiety caused by the war were the origin of his illness.

## 1918

The war makes life difficult in many ways. It is such a period of unrest. People leave their homes and let them, and the hotels are full – maids are unsettled, munition and other workers getting such high wages.

There are no end of marriages, before the men go out, or when they are home on leave.

Rationing is difficult and the strain and sadness of the war make people's tempers uncertain. It is difficult to get work done, and incompetent people are doing things.

Compulsory rationing has been in for about a month now and is working very well. We are rationed for sugar (1/2 lb a head), butter or

margarine 4 oz each, meat one shilling and three pence worth (which is about 3/4 of a lb) and 4 oz of bacon.

There are four coupons for meat on each card, only three of which can be used at the butcher's so the five of us put our coupons together and get a Sunday joint to the value of 6/3-, and we either get sausages or bacon with the other coupons. For five coupons you get 1 lb 14 oz of sausages.

Just before the rationing came in you would see queues of 200 or 300 people waiting to get margarine or butter. They would stand for hours.

**October 24:** I have written nothing in this book since May 12, and since then we have had a great sorrow. Our darling mother left us in the early morning of June 25. I will not write about it here.

She was only taken ill at 9.20 on the Monday evening, and died at 3 o'clock on Tuesday morning. George and I got down at 11.30 and we watched her peacefully passing away. I was so thankful that there was no raid.

At the end of the October, the Germans asked for an armistice, and that hostilities might cease during the consideration of the terms.

This last request was refused, and everyone much hoped that the German army would be thoroughly conquered before the terms were arranged and General Foch did go ahead. It was thrilling day after day to read the papers.

**November 11:** Bang went a maroon somewhere near. People thought it was an air raid. Then more maroons went, and we knew it was 'peace' at last. In a very few minutes windows were thrown open, doors flew open and people crowded to the doors and windows.

A few called to us, for I think we were the only people out, 'Is it an air raid?' and we called, 'It's peace, peace.'

Flags suddenly appeared from windows and everyone began to laugh and talk, and the children to dance.

The next day, November 12, the order for shading lights was removed, so now one does not have to carefully close up every chink round the windows at a stated time, or see that one's blinds are carefully drawn. It is such a relief.

The food situation is much the same, and is not likely to vary much at present, nor are prices expected to come down much yet, but – the war is over!

# YOUNGEST SOLDIER SIGNED UP AGED 12

The youngest person to serve in the First World War was 12-year-old Private Sidney Lewis.

The well-built boy, having lied to recruitment officers about his age, enlisted in August 1915 and endured the horrors of the Western Front 10 months later.

During his time fighting on the front line, Sidney was awarded the Victory Medal and the British War Medal, but was sent home after his worried mother contacted Army officials.

Imperial War Museum staff confirmed Sidney, pictured, was the youngest fighting soldier after examining a bundle of family papers and a faded cutting from the Daily Mirror dated September 1916.

It revealed: "He joined the East Surreys at Kingston in August, 1915, when only 12 years old and fought on the Somme front for six weeks."

The article was accompanied by an undated photograph of him which was taken at Grantham, Lincolnshire, as he is thought to be awaiting his discharge.

"Sidney's mother, Fanny Lewis, was worried sick and wrote to officials with his birth certificate and within weeks he was sent home," says Richard van Emden, author of Boy Soldiers of the Great War.

"It's amazing to think he served on the Western Front for six weeks without the Army realising his true age."

Recruiting officers often turned a blind eye to underage recruits because of a chronic shortage of soldiers and Sidney, of Kingston-on-Thames, Surrey, was tall for his age.

Recrits had to be a minimum of just five feet three inches tall and Sidney was to grow to 6ft 2in when he reached adulthood.

Sidney survived the war and, when he was old enough, joined the Surrey police before running a pub called The George in Frant, near Tunbridge Wells, Kent.

Until recently, the youngest soldier was thought to be Lancashire boy Edward Barnett, who was just 13 when he was enlisted with the Manchester Regiment in May 1915.

Within a week he was kicked out after officials realised his real age.

However, the determined boy soldier re-enlisted the very next day in the 19th Manchester Regiment.

The teenager completed his training undetected and, when he was 13 years and 10 months old, was sent to France to join the 20th Manchester Regiment in December 1915.

He lasted almost four months fighting on the Western Front before he was brought home.

# BURNED ALIVE AS THEY HEADED OFF TO BATTLE

**More than 200 soldiers never made it to the battlefield after they were killed in Britain's worst ever railway disaster, writes Bob Paterson**

Main picture, the aftermath of the train crash in Quintinshill. Right, the Caledonian Railway engine which hauled the troop train involved in the disaster

**P**acked on a train, hundreds of soldiers must have feared what lay in store as they started their journey to the First World War battleground of Gallipoli.

What they could never have imagined is that so many of them would lose their lives on home soil.

On May 22, 1915, Quintinshill infamously grabbed the unwanted honour of being the location of Britain's worst railway disaster.

It was just after 7am when a troop train carrying a Royal Scots battalion smashed into a stationary passenger train at high speed near

Gretna. As the survivors tried to escape the fire which immediately engulfed their train they were hit again by a London to Glasgow express as it passed near the border town.

The accident claimed the lives of 227 people, all but 12 of them Royal Scots soldiers, with some 246 left wounded.

Local residents became unsung heroes battling against the odds to free the living and rescue the injured.

Among them was Andrew Sword, who told the Daily Record: "The first thing I did was to run to the rearmost side of the train. I heard voices, people shouting. One man cried, 'Help me out of here.' The voice came from a half-open window. I rushed up, seeing

# " THE FIRE WAS DREADFUL. IT WAS VERY NOTICEABLE THAT AMONG THE CRIES, THAT OF 'MOTHER! MOTHER!' WAS THE MOST FREQUENT "

a piece of wood on the way, and smashed the window. Another man came up and we pulled the passenger out. Through the same window we pulled another man and a third but he was injured.

"The next passenger I helped to rescue, for there were soldiers at hand now, was a man who had his back and both his legs broken. He cried out in agony when I only touched him. But we had to get him through the window in spite of his cries, for the flames were creeping up and would set him on fire. We got him out in time."

One of the first medics to arrive on the scene was Dr Taylor, who said: "The fire was dreadful. The carriages burned up like boxes of matches. We could see passengers being burned alive in the midst of the flames and could not help them.

"Now and then there were what appeared to be explosions of the gas cylinders, and with every explosion the flames increased. It was very noticeable that among the cries of the injured and dying, that of 'Mother! Mother!' was most frequent."

Some of the survivors of the accident which claimed the lives of 227 people, all but 12 of them Royal Scots soldiers, and left 246 wounded

Dr Edwards, who was also the full-back for the Watsonians rugby team, motored to the accident scene from Carlisle and amputated the legs of men pinned under the wreckage. On one occasion, in the presence of unexploded gas canisters and live bullets exploding everywhere due to the fire, he had to lie across a dead man to perform an amputation by sawing through a thigh bone.

Among the wounded was Peter Skea, a corporal in the 7th Royal Scots whose face and hands were severely burned.

He also suffered a broken leg which was left permanently shortened, and he was eventually awarded £125 in damages from Caledonian Railway. A number of bodies from the disaster were never recovered, having been wholly consumed by the fire.

Those that were recovered were buried together in a mass grave in Edinburgh's Rosebank Cemetery, where a memorial to the victims stands today. Four bodies, believed to be of children, were never identified or claimed and are buried in the Western Necropolis in Glasgow.

# Signalmen 'forgot about train on line'

Quintinshill was a passing loop on the Caledonian Railway just north of Gretna at the time of the disaster.

A passenger train from Carlisle was switched from the down main line onto the up main line and halted; effectively blocking the path of the oncoming troop train.

The troop train slammed into the stationary one and barely had the wreckage settled

when, 53 seconds later, the midnight express from Euston ploughed into the tangled mess.

The official report into the disaster laid the blame firmly at the feet of two signalmen – George Meakin and James Tinsley – who admitted they had simply forgotten about the local train occupying the main line.

A jury took just eight minutes

to find them guilty of culpable homicide due to gross neglect of their duties. Tinsley was jailed for three years, Meakin for 18 months.

The verdicts proved controversial at the time, due to the fact that neither man had previously caused any sort of harm, and that both would live with the accident on their consciences for the rest of their lives.

Australian gunners from the 9th Field Battery, stripped to the waist, operating an 18-pounder field gun at McCay's Hill on May 19, 1915, during the Battle of Gallipoli

**Above** Belgian cavalry in training in Campagne, France, on October 25, 1916

.................................

**Right** French troops firing over a wall in September 1914 as part of the attempt to halt the German advance on Paris

**Left**
Austrian
troops defend
a mountain
top during
the winter
campaign
on the
Montenegro
Front

**Below** French
soldiers
charge across
a field with
their rifles
raised in 1916

**Right** Montenegrin soldiers fighting the Austro-Hungarian invasion forces in the mountains in 1915

**Below** The camels of the Imperial Camel Corps, part of the Egyptian Expeditionary Force (EEF), return from watering on the Palestine Front during the Third Battle of Gaza in November 1917

**Left**
A messenger dog carrying orders arrives at a trench occupied by British soldiers in 1918

**Below right**
British artillery bombarding the German lines on the Somme battlefield in 1916

**Above** German prisoners of war captured during the Somme offensive

Pipers, believed to be from the Cameron Highlanders, marching
to the front line during the Battle of the Somme in July 1916

**Right** Royal Horse Artillery horses being watered in northern France in October 1914

**Below** Members of the Royal Garrison Artillery regiment loading up artillery shells on to a light railway trolley near Fricourt in the Somme in September 1916

**Left** A German dispatch dog taking messages to the front line during the German advance of January 1918

**Below** Italian troops with sledge dog teams during the Battle of the Isonzo in November 1917

British troops, flanked by two French soldiers, pose with captured German guns at their French base

Belgian artillerymen having a meal in 1915

A soldier next to the klaxon horn which warned against a gas attack on French trenches

The Crown Prince of Germany, left, studying a map with one of his officers during the Second Battle of Champagne, which took place from September 25 to November 6, 1915. The Allied advance forced the German Third and Fifth Armies, commanded by Generalleutnant Wilhelm in the Argonne sector, to withdraw along the Meuse River towards Belgium

**Right** These women were making pellets at a munitions factory in April 1918

**Below** Women workers filling bags with coke at a Cambridge gas works

British troops prepare to fire a trench-mortar from a captured German trench in Gommecourt, France, in March 1917

**Right** British soldiers loading ammunition on to a bus in London's Hyde Park in 1915

**Below** Belgian civil guards are seen manning a barricade across one of the roads leading into Brussels in August 1914

**Opposite** The French town of Senlis following a bombardment by German artillery during their advance on Paris in September 1914

**Right** A British airman holds a bomb in his hand, looks out of his aircraft and takes aim at his target in 1917

**Below** A Royal Flying Corps aircraft drops a torpedo towards its target in 1915

**Below right** A biplane takes off from the deck of the aircraft carrier HMS Argus in the Firth of Forth in 1918

French soldiers prepare observation kites for reconnaissance work over enemy lines in 1916

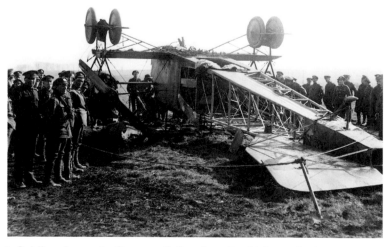

Soldiers inspect a German Gotha aircraft which crashed on British lines at the Western Front in 1918

# New weapon of war led to first battles in the sky

When the First World War broke out, the airplane was less than 11 years old.

Aircrafts of the day were slow, flimsy and could carry only a pilot and possibly one passenger. Initially, they were limited to spying on the enemy's activities and resources.

As aerial reconnaissance became more common, so the need to stop this became more crucial. Pilots tried to shoot at other planes using rifles and even pistols – a method that proved hopeless. It was Dutch aviator Anton Fokker who, working for the Germans, provided the solution for firing a machine gun through a propeller.

With the development of the fighter plane came the concept of 'dog fights'. Battles in the sky became common and great air 'aces' on all sides achieved celebrity status. In reality, new pilots rarely survived beyond the first few weeks of duty.

When the war started, bombing was crude – hand-held bombs were thrown over the side of planes. By the end of the war, specialised bomber aircrafts were developed.

Russia was the first to produce the first dedicated multi-engine bomber in the Sikorsky Ilya Muromets. Germany took a different approach by using Zeppelin airships which could carry a large cargo of explosives but became increasingly vulnerable as fighter planes became more advanced.

In Britain, in recognition of the growing importance of aerial combat, the Royal Air Force was founded on April 1, 1918.

On the whole, aerial warfare in the First World War did not inflict the kind of damage that bombing did in the Second World War. However, it certainly brought about the rapid development of the airplane, both in general and specifically as a weapon.

**Above** British airmen drop bombs from their plane in 1914

**Left** An aerial photograph captures the destruction in Belgium in August 1914

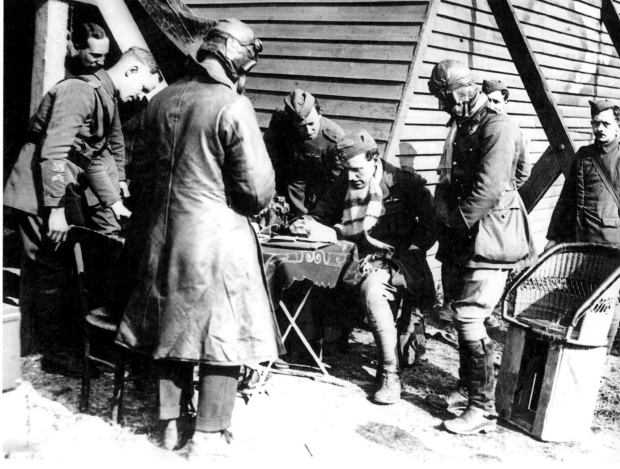

**Above**
Artillerymen setting the fuses for a bombardment of the German trenches on the Somme battlefield in August 1916

**Right** RAF pilots report the position of enemy troops on the Western Front in 1918

**Above** A Zeppelin airship flies over the ocean

**Left** British troops guard the wreckage of a German Gotha bomber after it was brought down by anti-aircraft fire close to Whitstable in December 1917

**Right** A female taxi driver takes money from a passenger in Eastbourne in 1917

**Below left** A wounded soldier recruiting on the streets of London in July 1915

**Below right** Women painting bill posters in Stratford in 1917

**Above** A shop is attacked during anti-German riots in London in 1915

**Left** Gas masks and other protective equipment were being made at this workshop in July 1916

Belgian artillerymen return fire during the siege of Antwerp in October 1914

**Below** Members of the Highland Light Infantry being inspected in Glasgow by Lieutenant-General Sir Reginald Pole-Carew

**Below** The offices of R. Ropner and Co, in Hartlepool, which were hit by a German shell fire during a raid by the German navy in December 1914

**Above**
A British gun crew on board HMS Falmouth looking at the sinking of the German ship Mainz, near the Heligoland islands, in August 1914

**Right** The aircraft carrier HMS Argus, pained in dazzle camouflage, with a Renown class battlecruiser in the distance

**Left**
Soldiers from the Duke of Cornwall's Light Infantry on the front line near Ypres with the regimental mascot in 1915

**Below left**
Kaiser Wilhelm II inspects a group of army doctors in a village close to the front during the Second Battle of Ypres in 1915

**Below right**
A female tram conductor employed during the First World War

**Above**
Munition
factory
workers
show off their
creations

**Right**
Women
gauging fuses
in April 1918

**Left** A German soldier guards three captured British men in April 1917

**Below** Dawn breaks as refugees make their way to Antwerp ahead of the advancing Germans in September 1914

Members of the Army Service Corps set up a roadside field kitchen which they named 'Hotel Cecil' in October 1914

**Right** British soldiers take cover in their rudimentary bivouacs, constructed from tarpaulins and fencing, in the French countryside

..............................

**Below** Members of the Army Service Corps hanging up their washing after a hard day's work

**Above**
A 15-year-old girl working in a barber's shop near Waterloo Station in London during the First World War

**Left** Prince Edward, the Prince of Wales, during a visit to the Curran Munitions Works in Cardiff in February 1918

American soldiers are given a demonstration of a tank's capabilities while preparing to go out to the Western Front in January 1918

**Above** British soldiers round up German POWs after an attack on the Hindenburg Line in 1918

**Right** Prime Minister David Lloyd George, centre, and French President Georges Clemenceau, standing beside him on the right, are pictured arriving at the Paris Peace Conference in 1919

**Above** The scene in Glasgow on November 11, 1918, with large crowds in George Square listening to Lord Provost Welsh

**Left** Howitzers lined up and ready for action on the Western Front during the final months of the war

**Above**
King George V and the Queen are pictured in their carriage in Hyde Park during the peace celebrations in July 1919

**Right** Winston Churchill, then the Secretary of State for War and Secretary of State for Air, is pictured with General John Pershing

**Far right** The victory march in London passes over Westminster Bridge

The scene on The Mall during the peace celebrations in London

# "WE SHALL HAVE TO FIGHT ANOTHER WAR AGAIN IN 25 YEARS' TIME"

Prime Minister David Lloyd George's grim prediction following the signing of the Treaty of Versailles, which imposed severe penalties on Germany, in 1919